all
you need
is
a good
BRAINWASHING

all
you need
is
a good
BRAINWASHING

DR. FRANK SUMMERFIELD

ɯ

WHITAKER
HOUSE

All Scripture quotations are taken from the King James Version of the Holy Bible.

ALL YOU NEED IS A GOOD BRAINWASHING

You may contact the author at:
Summerfield Ministries
P.O. Box 46891
Raleigh, NC 27620
phone: 919-834-1141
www.summerfieldministries.org

ISBN: 0-88368-771-2
Printed in the United States of America
© 2002 by Frank Summerfield

Whitaker House
30 Hunt Valley Circle
New Kensington, PA 15068
web site: www.whitakerhouse.com

Library of Congress Cataloging-in-Publication Data

Summerfield, Frank, 1950–
  All you need is a good brainwashing / by Frank Summerfield.
    p. cm.
ISBN 0-88368-771-2 (pbk. : alk. paper)
1. Success—Religious aspects—Christianity. 2. Thought and
thinking—Religious aspects—Christianity. I. Title.
BV4598.3 .S86 2002
248.4—dc21

                            2002006568

    1 2 3 4 5 6 7 8 9 10 11 12 / 10 09 08 07 06 05 04 03 02

Contents

Foreword

How refreshing it is to see a book discussing an area that affects everyone's lives—the mind. The majority of our problems—whether they're health-related, financial, marital, emotional, or any other area—can be traced back to that one source. And although many have written books on the power of the mind, the war in the mind, and the power of positive thinking, none have captured the essence of God's heart in quite the same way that Dr. Frank Summerfield does in this book. That's why *All You Need Is a Good Brainwashing* is so important to the body of Christ.

Dr. Summerfield ministers with a comprehensive understanding of God's Word. There are few people like him who can dig into the depths of Scripture and uncover pertinent biblical truths to help the people in society today. The self-reflective process you will go through as you read this book will undoubtedly assure your deliverance from what has been plaguing your mind.

As Dr. Summerfield says, *all you need is a good brainwashing!*

— Bishop George Bloomer
Author of *Authority Abusers;*
Crazy House, Sane House;
This Is War;
and *Witchcraft in the Pews*
Pastor of Bethel Worship Center
Durham, North Carolina

1

Realizing Where the War Is

1

Realizing Where the War Is

Can you picture this scenario? Two countries are at war, their armies engaged in fierce combat. Artillery and rifle fire are exchanged; shouts and the rumble of machinery deafen the camp. The fighting is fierce. The only problem is that one army is in one area, and the other is in a completely different place! How can one army win over the other if they're not even fighting at the same spot?

So many Spirit-filled believers and kingdom heirs go through life defeated and never fulfill their destinies because they don't know where the war is in their lives. They don't know where the battleground is. Many believe that their failures and defeats come from bad luck, bad timing, bad family background, and other negative circumstances. In actuality, they don't understand that their failures and defeats in life come as a result of losing the war in the mind. Some don't realize that there even is a war!

Make no mistake—there is a war, and you have an enemy.

♋ All You Need Is a Good Brainwashing

And the great dragon was cast out, that old serpent, called the Devil, and Satan, which deceiveth the whole world: he was cast out into the earth, and his angels were cast out with him. And I heard a loud voice saying in heaven, Now is come salvation, and strength, and the kingdom of our God, and the power of his Christ: for the accuser of our brethren is cast down, which accused them before our God day and night. And they overcame him by the blood of the Lamb, and by the word of their testimony; and they loved not their lives unto the death. Therefore rejoice, ye heavens, and ye that dwell in them. Woe to the inhabiters of the earth and of the sea! for the devil is come down unto you, having great wrath, because he knoweth that he hath but a short time. (Revelation 12:9–12)

The devil lost his fight in the heavens and got tossed out onto the earth. As a result, he's desperate to destroy the lives of God's highest creation—mankind. However, God sent Jesus to redeem mankind and empower us to defeat the devil!

The thief cometh not, but for to steal, and to kill, and to destroy: I am come that they might have life, and that they might have it more abundantly. (John 10:10)

Behold, I give unto you power to tread on serpents and scorpions, and over all the power of the enemy: and nothing shall by any means hurt you. (Luke 10:19)

Jesus gave us authority over all of Satan's power. So why are we still in a war? Satan knows that Jesus came so we could have life and have it more abundantly. Satan, on the other hand, comes to steal, kill, and destroy what Jesus has already died for us to have. If he can steal, kill, or destroy our concept of Jesus' finished work in our thought life, then he can steal from, kill, and destroy us. The only real weapon that Satan can use against us is deception. And deception begins in our minds, in our thought patterns.

Did you know that the human mind processes around 650,000 thoughts every twenty-four hours, some conscious and some subconscious? This gives the spiritual principalities and the rulers of the darkness of this world—the enemy— about 650,000 opportunities to explode deceptive missiles of doubt, fear, confusion, frustration, anxiety, worry, and other negative devices in your mental headquarters. If demons can deceive you into dwelling on these things, they gain a tremendous amount of control over your life. Their corrupt thoughts will negate the supernatural creative power that your mind possesses.

The apostle Paul talked about this war.

I find then a law, that, when I would do good, evil is present with me. For I delight in the law of God after the inward man: but I see another law in my members, warring against the law of my mind, and bringing me into captivity to the law of sin which is in my members. O wretched man that I am! who shall deliver me from the body of this death? I thank God through Jesus Christ our Lord. So then with the mind I myself serve the law of God; but with the flesh the law of sin.

(Romans 7:21–25)

Paul said that there was a war against the mind that was trying to bring him into sin. So we can see very clearly that these angry enemies are desperately trying to deceive our thought patterns in order to destroy our lives. We're in a war, and the war is in our minds. If we're going to win this war, we need to fight it at the right place! We must set up a strong Word-governed defense system that's prepared for attack twenty-four hours a day. We must do what Peter said in 1 Peter 1:13:

> *Wherefore gird up the loins of your mind, be sober, and hope to the end for the grace that is to be brought unto you at the revelation of Jesus Christ.*

In order to be able to resist the enemy's attack against your mind and your thought life, you must get a good "Holy-Ghost-Word-of-God" brainwashing daily. Now, the world considers brainwashing to be a negative thing; to them it means a person's mind is being dominated or heavily influenced by someone or something else. But, in the positive sense, you can accomplish all that God has for you and fulfill your destiny when you allow the Word of God to influence your thinking! All you need is a good brainwashing by the Word of God.

> *Husbands, love your wives, even as Christ also loved the church, and gave himself for it; that he might sanctify and cleanse it with **the washing of water by the word**, that he might present it to himself a glorious church, not having spot, or wrinkle, or any such thing; but that it should be holy and without blemish.*
> (Ephesians 5:25–27, emphasis added)

> *Now ye are clean through the word which I have spoken unto you.* (John 15:3)

Your mind must be washed from whatever deceptive thoughts have been planted there by the enemy to take you out of your God-ordained prosperous destiny. Prosperity includes spiritual or physical health and well-being. You accomplish this cleansing by daily renewing your mind with the anointed Word of God (which, as Proverbs 4:22 says, is *"life unto those that find* [it], *and health to all their flesh"*). It's the continual hearing of the Word of God that causes the cleansing and renewing of your mind to take place.

> *And be renewed in the spirit of your mind.*
> (Ephesians 4:23)

> *And be not conformed to this world: but be ye trans-formed by the renewing of your mind, that ye may prove what is that good, and acceptable, and perfect, will of God.* (Romans 12:2)

Ephesians 4:23 shows us that the mind has a spirit that only the Word of God can renew as we are continually exposed to the Word over and over again. Based on Romans 12:2, we can see that our lives can be transformed only if our minds are renewed.

It's interesting to note that the word *transformed* in Romans 12:2 comes from the Greek word *metamorphoō*, which, according to *Vine's*, means going through "a complete change which, under the power of God, will find expression in character and conduct."[1] In other words, we will change from earthly to supernatural, becoming Christ-natured. It's also interesting to note that the Greek word for *"renewing"* in this same verse is *anakainōsis*, which denotes "the adjust-ment of the moral and spiritual vision and thinking to the mind of God, which is designed to have a transforming effect upon the life."[2] You could say that it will make a person dif-ferent from his past! So a good brainwashing with the Word of God is how you transform into someone who thinks, acts, and talks like Jesus Christ—a Christian!

⚘ All You Need Is a Good Brainwashing

This is how you win the battle in your mind. When your mind is saturated or renewed with the anointed Word regarding a situation or promise, then you can stand firm and resist whatever deceptive thoughts the devil sends you regarding that issue. *"And ye shall know the truth, and the truth shall make you free"* (John 8:32). Daily mind renewal empowers you to stand against the attack or wiles of the devil:

> *Finally, my brethren, be strong in the Lord, and in the power of his might. Put on the whole armour of God, that ye may be able to stand against the wiles of the devil. For we wrestle not against flesh and blood, but against principalities, against powers, against the rulers of the darkness of this world, against spiritual wickedness in high places.* (Ephesians 6:10–12)

These spiritual forces bombard your approximate 650,000 thoughts a day as often as they possibly can to create confusion, havoc, fear, doubt, worry, anxiety, depression, and every negative emotion available—all in order to make you abort your own prosperous destiny. They know that you are predestined for great and mighty works, and they will do all they can to prevent those things from coming to pass.

The first step to winning this war and positioning yourself for success and victory is to realize that the war the enemy is waging against you is in your mind. You're not going to win if you try to fight the enemy at the wrong battlefield!

The next step is to begin to renew your mind to what God's Word says, as we briefly discussed earlier. If you can discipline and equip yourself to make your thought patterns become like God's, you can win the war being waged against you. The final result is a mental cleansing or a *good brainwashing.* When your mind is full of the Word of God and you think like He does, there isn't anything He wants you to do that you can't do!

Once your mind is purged from the enemy's negative thought patterns by the anointed Word, you can do what Philippians 4:8 says:

> *Finally, brethren, whatsoever things are true, whatsoever things are honest, whatsoever things are just, whatsoever things are pure, whatsoever things are lovely, whatsoever things are of good report; if there be any virtue, and if there be any praise, think on these things.*

When you have changed your thought patterns and renewed your mind to think like God does, your mind will begin to conceive the supernatural things that 1 Corinthians 2:9 talks about: *"Eye hath not seen, nor ear heard, neither have entered into the heart of man, the things which God hath prepared for them that love him."*

It all begins, however, when you realize that the war is in your mind!

> *For though we walk in the flesh, we do not war after the flesh: (for the weapons of our warfare are not carnal, but mighty through God to the pulling down of strong holds;) casting down imaginations, and every high thing that exalteth itself against the knowledge of God, and bringing into captivity every thought to the obedience of Christ.* (2 Corinthians 10:3–5)

Again, this passage makes it very clear that we are in mental warfare and that our weapons include the Spirit of

✐ All You Need Is a Good Brainwashing

God and His Word, which enable us to cast down the wicked, deceptive imaginations that rob us of what God has ordained for us.

It's important to note that the word *"imaginations"* in the passage of 2 Corinthians 10 comes from the Greek word *logismos*, which means reasonings or computations[3]—in this case, contrary or hostile to the Gospel. In other words, the imaginations we are battling are thoughts that are against the anointed, life-giving Word that declares the promises of God, that declares your deliverance, victory, and prosperity.

Many attacks—even a physical attack—start in your mind. Sometimes you think you're sick before you're really sick. Don't even try to fight this battle using your own natural mind. It won't work. As important as the mind is and as powerful as it is, it cannot provide for its own health. No, it takes the spiritual, life-giving Word of God. Unfortunately, we don't give our minds the same food and attention we do our flesh—but they need it, too!

The mind—and what is in the mind—is the key. When sickness comes, the attack isn't really against the body; it is against everything in the Word of God about divine healing. When financial lack comes, it is an attack on everything the Word has to say about prosperity. When depression comes, it is an attack on what God's Word says about joy. When fear and doubt come, it is an attack on what God's Word says about faith. We have divine health, prosperity, all courage, joy, and faith through Jesus and the Word. The attack comes to take possession of what is in your mind—what you confess, believe, have faith in, and possess.

That situation or those circumstances come to attack the Word and the knowledge of God you hold in your mind. In a natural war, in order to invade a country, the enemy must go to that country. The devil does the same thing. He invades your mind because that is where the Word resides. Don't let him have it! Hold on to that Word. Fight for that Word. You can't win in life without it. If the enemy says you're broke, say, "Second Corinthians 8:9 says, 'Jesus became poor that I might be rich.'" If he says you can't, say, "Philippians 4:13 says, *I can do all things through Christ.*'" If he says you're sick, say, "Isaiah 53:5 says, 'By His stripes I am healed.'" Speak the Word! Fear, doubt, worry, resentment, and bad thoughts of the past support the principalities and wicked rulers of darkness that want to drain you of the Christ-nature inside you. Thoughts of old failures and disappointments feed these spiritual principalities. Philippians 3:13 says to forget *"those things which are behind."* The enemy wants to marry your mind. Your mind should be married to the Word of God.

Realize where the war is being waged against you and start fighting the good fight of faith, resisting the enemy with a Word-filled, faith-filled, and Word-cleansed mind.

There is another spiritual defense that we can use against the enemy in the war against our minds:

Forasmuch then as Christ hath suffered for us in the flesh, arm yourselves likewise with the same mind: for he that hath suffered in the flesh hath ceased from sin.
(1 Peter 4:1)

Here the apostle Peter told us that we must be armed in our minds with the same mind Jesus had and has. Paul made a similar statement in Philippians 2:5: *"Let this mind be in you, which was also in Christ Jesus."* What was Jesus' mind? Look at how He handled the spiritual warfare right before He faced His biggest trial in His earthly ministry: He spent time in intense, persistent prayer. (See Matthew 26:36–45 and Luke 22:39–46.) It was during this time that He got His major break-through in the Spirit. He girded His mind and won the war in His mind before He went to the cross. Jesus' mind was armed with prayer and the Word of God, and our minds must be armed in the same way.

Sincere, persistent, intense prayer will gird our minds and enable us to win the war that is waged against us. Combined with the anointed Word of God, such prayer will arm our minds with what we need to win the war against the enemy.

The war that's being waged against you is in your mind. God has provided you with a defense: keeping your brain washed daily with the anointed Word of God, prayer, the Holy Spirit, and godly leadership. (We'll discuss the latter in the next chapter.) Don't let the wicked devices of the enemy defile and corrupt your thoughts. Corrupt thoughts will negate the supernatural creative power your mind possesses.

Now that you realize where the war is, start defending your mind with a good brainwashing on a consistent, regular basis, and you'll begin to experience the victory that Jesus Christ died for you to have.

Don't be a victim when you can be a victor. Recognize the importance of winning the mental war, and discipline your mind with the anointed Word and prayer!

Notes

[1] W. E. Vine, *Vine's Expository Dictionary of Old & New Testament Words* (Nashville: Thomas Nelson, Inc., 1997), 1160, "transform, transfigure."

[2] Vine, *Expository Dictionary*, 950–951, "renew, renewing."

[3] James Strong, *Strong's Hebrew and Greek Dictionaries* (Cedar Rapids, Iowa: Parsons Technology, Inc., Electronic Edition STEP Files © 1998), #G3053.

2

Don't Let Carnality Kill You

2

Don't Let Carnality Kill You

Out of the entire arsenal that the enemy has at his disposal, probably the one device that can most destroy our lives is carnality. *Carnality* is a word that has its origin in the Greek word *sarx*, which refers to the "nature of flesh" in that it is "sensual, controlled by animal appetites, governed by human nature, instead of by the Spirit of God."[1]

As we consider this definition, it becomes clear that there is a lower order and nature that tends to exist in our minds when we are not led and controlled by the Holy Spirit. Without going into a deep theological discussion, there are two forces vying for control of our minds: the carnal nature and our reborn spirit-nature, the inner man, which is controlled by the Holy Spirit. One follows the appetite of the flesh; the other follows the principles and truth in the life-giving Word of God.

The Holy Spirit, according to John 16:13, guides us into all truth: *"Howbeit when he, the Spirit of truth, is come, he will guide you into all truth: for he shall not speak of himself;*

but whatsoever he shall hear, that shall he speak: and he will show you things to come." The Holy Spirit is our guide, companion, helper, advocate, and direct link to our heavenly Father. When our minds are submitted to Him and daily washed with the Word, then we find life. But when we allow our minds to be controlled by our carnal nature, we open our lives to destruction by a process of deterioration.

There is a constant conflict between our new spiritual nature and the old carnal nature, which fights the will and purpose of God. In fact, Romans 8:7 says that the carnal mind and nature is the very enemy of God—and that means it's your enemy as well. You can't afford to allow carnality to control you because it will take you out of the will of God and eventually kill you. Carnality has a way of convincing you to follow the desires and appetites of the flesh instead of the direction of the life-giving Spirit. The end result is disobedience to God and violation of His spiritual laws.

A careful look at Romans 8:4–9 reveals how carnality can lead to death and destruction.

That the righteousness of the law might be fulfilled in us, who walk not after the flesh, but after the Spirit. For they that are after the flesh do mind the things of the flesh; but they that are after the Spirit the things of the Spirit. For to be carnally minded is death; but to be spiritually minded is life and peace. Because the carnal mind is enmity against God: for it is not subject to the law of God, neither indeed can be. So then they that are in the flesh cannot please God. But ye are not in the flesh, but in the Spirit, if so be that the Spirit of God dwell in you. Now if any man have not the Spirit of Christ, he is none of his.

July 2, 2010

To: J. Dening   A. Mone   cc: M. Green
    T. Dumbar   K. Morgan
    F. Elias   T. Newell
    R. Endicott   C. R. Porter
    P. Fineberg   C. Rider
    M. Maniguet   M. Von Itter

From: Bob Sanders

Subject: Loaned Books, DVDs, Videos Etc.

Please help me get back the items on loan to you. I suggest that you put the item(s) in a sealed bag or envelope, with my name on the bag/envelope, and put the bag on the floor under the mail boxes at Hydewood. If you cannot find the item(s) loaned to you, you may have returned the item(s) and I did not check the return box on my loan list. I trust the loaned item(s) were helpful to you. Thank you for your attention to this request.

Loaned Item(s):

( ) Book: <u>Already Gone</u>: Why your Kids Will quit church and what you can do about it by Ken Ham & Britt Beemer with Todd Hillard, 2009

( ) Book: <u>Fish out of Water</u> by Abby Nye, 2007   (over)

( ) Book: <u>Thinking Straight in a Crooked World</u>, by Gary DeMar 2001

If you and Nadia have not finished any or all of these books, keep them longer; also, if you would like to loan them to friends, you can do that.

I have replaced all three books for my use.

<u>Note</u>: Recently, I purchased the DVD <u>Already Gone</u>, featuring Ken Ham; there is very little in this DUD from the book, <u>Already Gone</u>. Pastor Maniquet had this DVD or you can borrow my DVD if you would like to see it.

When you were born again, your spirit was reborn, but your body, your flesh, was not. So your carnal nature continually cries out for attention and gratification. It takes a tremendous amount of self-discipline on your part to follow the Spirit of God and the Word of God rather than your flesh. Your flesh will continually try to dominate your life with suggestions and even temptations to violate the laws of the Spirit of life in Christ Jesus. That's why Paul talked so much about buffeting the body and subduing it.

However, we have a promise in the Word of God that, when we meditate on it and change our thinking to match it, it gives us victory over the flesh! Romans 8:2 says, *"For the law of the Spirit of life in Christ Jesus hath made me free from the law of sin and death."* Jesus' death and resurrection freed us from the control of the law of sin and death! At the same time, the enemy continually uses the carnal nature, which is under the control of the law of sin and death, to try and bring our minds back under subjection to the flesh. So if we don't know the truth that we are freed from it, then we can easily get caught in the trap of the enemy.

Notice also what verses 12–13 say:

Therefore, brethren, we are debtors, not to the flesh, to live after the flesh. For if ye live after the flesh, ye shall die: but if ye through the Spirit do mortify the deeds of the body, ye shall live.

These verses reiterate the fact that we've been freed from the lower carnal nature of the flesh and do not have to be controlled by its influence. Every time we're presented with an issue or thought, we actually choose whether we will follow the carnal flesh nature or the Spirit. Meditate on these

27

verses and renew your mind to the truth! You're free! If you will follow the Spirit, you will mortify, or put to death, the deeds or works of the flesh. When you allow the Holy Spirit to influence and control your mind, you can avoid the pitfalls that the carnal nature tries to lead you into.

Again, all it takes is a good brainwashing to cleanse your mind from defiled and carnal thoughts. When you daily wash your mind with the Word of God, when you daily spend time in prayer and follow the leading of the Spirit, you will win the war against carnality in your mind.

As we've mentioned before, we don't win the battle in our minds with carnal weapons, but with spiritual weapons.

> *For though we walk in the flesh, we do not war after the flesh: (for the weapons of our warfare are not carnal, but mighty through God to the pulling down of strong holds;) casting down imaginations, and every high thing that exalteth itself against the knowledge of God, and bringing into captivity every thought to the obedience of Christ.* (2 Corinthians 10:3–5)

Clearly, we see that we win this mental battle with spiritual weapons—the promises of God. We are to cast down every thought and imagination that is contrary to those promises and make them obedient to the knowledge of the Word of God. However, there's one thing I want to point out: Casting down *every* thought and imagination requires a lot of diligence and effort on our part!

The greatest obstacle we face in our battle to defeat carnality is our own lack of self-discipline. We must force ourselves to think spiritually even when the attack that is confronting us is natural or earthly. We must renew our minds on a daily basis to think spiritually in order not to let carnality kill us.

Without daily renewal by the Word, you set yourself up to be a victim. God has ordained you to be a victor, not a victim, but you must win the mental battles daily. In addition to meditation on the Word, prayer, and following the Spirit, there is something else you can do to help yourself in this fight: You can associate with people who can speak a life-challenging and life-changing word into your mind.

In other words, you need to have a prophetically driven "priest" (shepherd/pastor) who will speak truth to you, as Malachi 2:5–7 talks about. At the same time, you must also be willing to submit yourself under such anointed leadership and allow the truth that they speak to drive out the lies, fear, doubt, and carnality from your mind! Joshua is a good example of this type of leadership:

And Moses spake unto the LORD, saying, Let the LORD, the God of the spirits of all flesh, set a man over the congregation, which may go out before them, and which may go in before them, and which may lead them out, and which may bring them in; that the congregation of the LORD be not as sheep which have no shepherd. And the LORD said unto Moses, Take thee Joshua the son of Nun, a man in whom is the spirit, and lay thine hand upon him; and set him before Eleazar the priest, and before all the congregation; and give him a charge in their sight. And thou shalt put some of thine honour upon him, that all the congregation of the children of Israel may be obedient. And he shall stand before Eleazar the priest, who shall ask counsel for him after the judgment of Urim before the LORD: at his word shall they go out, and at his word they shall come in, both he, and all the children of Israel with him, even all the congregation. And Moses did as the LORD commanded him: and he took Joshua, and set him before Eleazar the priest, and before all the congregation: and he laid his hands upon him, and gave him a charge, as the LORD commanded by the hand of Moses.

(Numbers 27:15–23)

We all need people who can speak life-changing, mind-renewing, spiritual truth into our minds and spirits. It is so important to have spiritual leadership with a word to go in and out of the affairs of life so your mind can stay washed and cleansed—and catch you if you fall victim to carnality. A Word-washed mind is a clean mind—one that can stand up against the attacks that come from the principalities, spiritual wickedness, rulers of the darkness, and deceptive devices of Satan.

Let me speak to leaders and shepherds for a moment. Even though you're a leader, you too need others who can speak a spiritually sound and anointed word into your life to help keep your mind renewed, cleansed, and free. Many good spiritual leaders have fallen victim to carnality because they failed to keep themselves exposed to a fresh, anointed, and cleansing word from someone in spiritual authority who could speak to their weary minds. Leaders, just like everyone else, can grow weary and fatigued and eventually fall into carnality. You must constantly check yourself to determine if weariness and battle fatigue have allowed the ever-busy demon of carnality to invade or penetrate your thought patterns.

Don't get so caught up in the tasks and challenges that face leaders that you forget to follow the Spirit as well.

Romans 8:14 says, *"For as many as are led* [Greek, *agō*— driven, induced, carried[2]] *by the Spirit of God, they are the sons of God."* If you're not being led by the ever-ready-to-help Spirit of God, eventually you will fall victim to carnality—and possibly sins that you'll greatly regret afterward.

Leaders, please be diligent! We leaders carry a great responsibility. Not only can our own sins cause us to lose our visions and destinies, but they also affect the visions and destinies of those whom we lead.

We all must come to the realistic conclusion that either we are going to be controlled by the Holy Spirit and let the Word of God brainwash us or we will become victims of carnality, causing disaster for ourselves and possibly others.

The real purpose of carnality's attacks is to nullify what you have inside you—your purpose and destiny in God. As a born-again child of God, you have the Spirit of God inside you. The attack comes so that you fail to tap into and identify with the inner spirit man, reborn after the image of Christ, especially at a crucial time when you need the supernatural strength, patience, courage, or faith that comes from the presence of the Spirit of God in your life. You have to be sharp enough to know that these attacks come to cause disaster in all three parts of your being—your spirit, soul, and body. Attacks of carnality usually come gradually as we travel along the highway of life. And just as a natural highway has signs to warn you of changes that may cause you problems, so the Spirit of God sends warning signs of impending spiritual disaster.

These warning signs are there to prevent you from going in the wrong direction and getting into an accident. Keep in mind that these warnings will come from inside you; they are not external. You need to know yourself well enough to see them. If you don't see the sign that reads "Lane Ends Ahead," for example, you won't change lanes. You probably won't even slow down. If you ignore signs like a runny nose or a scratchy throat, you may end up in bed for a week. You get signs from your body, your finances, your marriage, your children, and every other area. But when you backslide, sin, or get into fear, doubt, or worry, you've failed to see a sign that God posted for you. Then you become vulnerable—because not only has God seen you miss the sign, but the rulers of the kingdom of darkness also have seen you miss it, too.

When fear takes over or when anxiety and depression take over, you've missed a sign. When financial problems take over, you've missed a sign. When your marriage ends in divorce, you've missed a sign. When your child returns home with a police officer, you've missed a sign. The principalities start off slowly by asking, "What if...?" "What if God doesn't?" "What if God won't?" Before they ask those questions in your mind, you must not only believe that He will, but also confess that He already has! We must always trust God and believe in His Word.

Ephesians 6:10–18 explicitly instructs us to put on the whole armor of God so we can stand against the wiles of the devil. *"Wiles"* originally meant devices and tricks. Every time you miss a warning sign, the enemy works that much harder at tricking you into leaving the Spirit of God behind. We must be *"strong in the Lord, and in the power of his might"* like Ephesians 6:10 says. Putting on the whole armor of God involves your prayer life, your fasting life, your study life, and your relationship with God as a whole. Prayer, fasting, study, and meditation renew your mind with the things you need in order to stand against the devil. The principalities and rulers of the darkness of this world work to gradually influence your mind with the wrong things in an attempt to penetrate the armor of God. These signs let you know that your armor has been penetrated.

It is important to take the time to feed the mind the right things, to renew your mind to the Word of God. The mind is the control center for the entire body. It is the first site of a warning sign for spiritual disaster. Learn to read your mind and to control it—it's where the battle is won.

Following are five warning signs of spiritual disaster. (There may be others.) If you see one or more of these in your life, take heed. God is trying to save you.

1. **Pride.** Pride is the first warning sign because it usually either leads you or blinds you to the others. When you are in pride, you think too highly of yourself to hear the correction God sends from godly authority. You resist criticism and any advice given in love. I recommend that you read Daniel 4 to see what happened to King Nebuchadnezzar when he got into pride. Proverbs 16:18 says, *"Pride goeth before destruction."* First Peter 5:5 says that *"God resisteth the proud,"* while Romans 12:3 instructs us *"not to think of* [ourselves] *more highly than* [we] *ought to think; but to think soberly, according as God hath dealt to every man the measure of faith."*

2. **Murmuring and complaining.** Pride usually leads to murmuring and complaining when certain things rub you the wrong way. For example, you might start

thinking negatively toward the person who corrects you or tries to guide you in the right direction. Numbers 13–14 describes the results of Israel's moaning and complaining about Moses. You don't want to end up in the same position. Also take heed to how Aaron and Miriam fared in Numbers 12. Finally, remember that Philippians 2:14 says to *"do all things without murmurings and disputings."*

3. **Loss of a desire to read the Word.** A decrease in your appetite for studying the Word of God is a sure sign of a spiritual fall. A person who is in pride and already murmuring and complaining will run from the truth in the Word. This is the exact opposite of what you need to do to avoid disaster. The Word won't work for you unless you have an appetite for it and enjoy it. Read Psalm 56:4: *"In God I will praise his word, in God I have put my trust; I will not fear what flesh can do unto me."* Paul also knew the importance of studying the Word of God. He told Timothy in 1 Timothy 4:13 to *"give attendance to reading."* He said in 2 Timothy 2:15, *"Study to show thyself approved unto God."* We must meditate in the Word to make it work for us.

4. **Loss of a desire to attend church.** Going to church becomes a chore. You no longer enjoy it. It feels like something you have to do out of obligation. It becomes hard, and you begin to be habitually late. Other things start to take precedence. The psalmist's attitude about church should be our model. David said in Psalm 26:8, *"Lord, I have loved the habitation of thy house."* In Psalm 27:4 he wrote, *"One thing*

have I desired of the LORD, that will I seek after; that I may dwell in the house of the LORD all the days of my life, to behold the beauty of the LORD, and to inquire in his temple." In Psalm 122:1, he said, *"I was glad when they said unto me, Let us go into the house of the LORD."* Hebrews 10:25 instructs us not to forsake *"the assembling of ourselves together,"* while the next verse suggests that forsaking church will lead to willful sin.

5. **A lackluster prayer life.** A limited prayer life or lack of craving for prayer is another warning sign. Your spirit should crave and be satisfied with prayer even if a situation does not immediately change. According to Jude 20, praying in the Spirit builds up your faith. We need the Holy Spirit to be active in our lives. *"Likewise the Spirit also helpeth our infirmities: for we know not what we should pray for as we ought: but the Spirit itself maketh intercession for us with groanings which cannot be uttered"* (Romans 8:26). Ephesians 6:18 says we should pray *"always with all prayer and supplication in the Spirit, and watching thereunto with all perseverance and supplication for all saints."* Jesus told His disciples that *"men ought always to pray, and not to faint"* (Luke 18:1), while Paul told the church to *"pray without ceasing"* (1 Thessalonians 5:17).

Fill your mind with the Word of God and let His Spirit lead you. Pray and fast; be disciplined in your walk; and listen to the godly leadership over your life. Remember, Romans 8:6 says, *"To be carnally minded is death; but to be spiritually minded is life and peace."* Death is a spiritual disaster. But your mind, filled with the Word of God and governed by a heart filled with the Spirit of God, will keep you in *"perfect peace"* (Isaiah 26:3).

Notes

[1] W. E. Vine, *Vine's Expository Dictionary of Old & New Testament Words* (Nashville: Thomas Nelson, Inc., 1997), 161, "carnal, carnally."

[2] James Strong, *Strong's Hebrew and Greek Dictionaries* (Cedar Rapids, Iowa: Parsons Technology, Inc., Electronic Edition STEP Files © 1998), #G71.

3

Tearing Down the Walls of Limitations

3

Tearing Down the Walls of Limitations

D id you know that your own mind can imprison you? All around you are only walls. Above the walls you see blue sky, puffy white clouds, and the tops of lush trees all around. You can even hear the singing of birds. But inside your four walls is nothing but dirt. How does this happen?

Gideon found himself in a similar situation.

And the hand of Midian prevailed against Israel: and because of the Midianites the children of Israel made them the dens which are in the mountains, and caves, and strong holds. And so it was, when Israel had sown, that the Midianites came up, and the Amalekites, and the children of the east, even they came up against them; and they encamped against them, and destroyed the increase of the earth, till thou come unto Gaza, and left no sustenance for Israel, neither sheep, nor ox, nor ass. For they came up with their cattle and their

*tents, and they came as grasshoppers for multitude; for
both they and their camels were without number: and
they entered into the land to destroy it. And Israel was
greatly impoverished because of the Midianites; and
the children of Israel cried unto the LORD....And there
came an angel of the LORD, and sat under an oak which
was in Ophrah, that pertained unto Joash the Abiezrite:
and his son Gideon threshed wheat by the winepress,
to hide it from the Midianites. And the angel of the LORD
appeared unto him, and said unto him, The LORD is with
thee, thou mighty man of valour. And Gideon said unto
him, Oh my Lord, if the LORD be with us, why then is all
this befallen us? and where be all his miracles which
our fathers told us of, saying, Did not the LORD bring us
up from Egypt? but now the LORD hath forsaken us, and
delivered us into the hands of the Midianites. And the
LORD looked upon him, and said, Go in this thy might,
and thou shalt save Israel from the hand of the Midianites: have not I sent thee? And he said unto him, Oh my
Lord, wherewith shall I save Israel? behold, my family
is poor in Manasseh, and I am the least in my father's
house. And the LORD said unto him, Surely I will be with
thee, and thou shalt smite the Midianites as one man.*
(Judges 6:2–6, 11–16)

Gideon and the Israelites had become victims of their
own disobedience and rebellion against the Lord. With all
the raids and attacks from the Midianites, they reduced
their thinking to the four walls of poverty and "woe is
me." In other words, they couldn't see past their low self-
esteem and impoverished condition. Yet God called Gideon
a *"mighty man of valour"*! Gideon had the potential and the
supernatural ability within him to tear down those walls of
limitations not only for his life but also for the lives of others.
He simply didn't know it.

Take stock of your life right now. Are you surrounded by lack, insufficiency, poverty, and walls of opposing forces and factors that seem to imprison you to a life of limitation? Do you suffer from low self-esteem or low self-worth? Do you lack self-confidence? Do you see yourself as a grasshopper, as a "nothing-nobody going nowhere"? Do you tend to spend what money you earn haphazardly with no specific disciplined disbursement plan (written budget)? If you answered yes to any or all of these questions, then you've got some mental walls of limitations that need to come down. Your mind needs a serious overhauling and restructuring so you can start tearing down those walls. Gideon had that ability in him, and so do you! All you need to do is get a brand-new understanding, from a biblical perspective, of God's unlimited thoughts, plans, desires, and purposes for your life. Beyond those walls lie your destiny!

So many Christians fail to realize that we serve an unlimited God who has given us an unlimited Savior with unlimited power. God frankly declares in Jeremiah 32:27, *"Behold, I am the LORD, the God of all flesh: is there any thing too hard for me?"* There is nothing God can't do—and He has given us the same potential. Jesus said to His followers:

> *If ye have faith as a grain of mustard seed, ye shall say unto this mountain, Remove hence to yonder place; and it shall remove; and nothing shall be impossible unto you.* (Matthew 17:20)

Do you realize the ramifications of that statement? Jesus was positioning us as joint heirs with Him, according to Romans 8:17, by saying *"nothing shall be impossible unto you."* Then where do these walls of limitations come from if our

All You Need Is a Good Brainwashing

Savior declared no limitations for our lives? Friend, the limitations are usually self-imposed; they are the result of what we have allowed to be set up in our minds. They are the result of swallowing the lies the enemy has told us. In order to tear down those walls, we must release our minds and thoughts to unlimited dimensions. As 1 Peter 4:1 says, we must arm ourselves with the same mind that Jesus had; as Philippians 2:5 says, we must let the unlimited mind of Jesus Christ operate in us: *"Let this mind be in you, which was also in Christ Jesus."*

In short, *all we need is a good brainwashing*—we need to renew our minds to what God has proclaimed over us in the anointed Word!

Many people fail naturally and spiritually because they allow ungodly, unbiblical thinking to clutter their minds with limitations and barriers that keep them from confidently releasing the power of the unlimited Jesus Christ who works in them. They fail to realize that He who lives in them is, as Ephesians 3:20 says, *"able to do exceeding abundantly above all that we ask or think, according to* [His] *power that worketh in us."*

It has never been God's intention for you to fail, lose, or be stuck in the pit of lack with walls of limitations around your life. To help you start renewing your mind, here are some verses that proclaim God's intention for you. Focus your mind on these!

> *Beloved, I wish above all things that thou mayest prosper and be in health, even as thy soul prospereth. For I rejoiced greatly, when the brethren came and testified of the truth that is in thee, even as thou walkest in the truth.* (3 John 2–3)

For I know the thoughts that I think toward you, saith the Lord, thoughts of peace, and not of evil, to give you an expected end. Then shall ye call upon me, and ye shall go and pray unto me, and I will hearken unto you. And ye shall seek me, and find me, when ye shall search for me with all your heart. And I will be found of you, saith the Lord: and I will turn away your captivity, and I will gather you from all the nations, and from all the places whither I have driven you, saith the Lord; and I will bring you again into the place whence I caused you to be carried away captive. (Jeremiah 29:11–14)

Let them shout for joy, and be glad, that favour my righteous cause: yea, let them say continually, Let the Lord be magnified, which hath pleasure in the prosperity of his servant. (Psalm 35:27)

Blessed is the man that walketh not in the counsel of the ungodly, nor standeth in the way of sinners, nor sitteth in the seat of the scornful. But his delight is in the law of the Lord; and in his law doth he meditate day and night. And he shall be like a tree planted by the rivers of water, that bringeth forth his fruit in his season; his leaf also shall not wither; and whatsoever he doeth shall prosper. (Psalm 1:1–3)

Are you constantly meditating in the Word of God day and night? Is God's Word your delight? Constant, diligent attention to the Word of God will give you *"length of days, and long life, and peace,"* and *"favour and good understanding in the sight of God and man"* (Proverbs 3:2, 4).

Are you even aware that it gives God pleasure when you prosper beyond the limited boundaries that the world and circumstances tend to place around your life?

ℰ All You Need Is a Good Brainwashing

Again I ask, Are you literally walking on a daily basis in the pure truth of God's Word? Are you consistently applying its principles to your daily life? Is your mind renewed to what God thinks and says? Are you really seeking God with all your heart at every opportunity you get through prayer, fasting, and study? Or are you walking in the enemy's lies of depression, discouragement, and low self-esteem? Are you spending your time in a lot of useless, idle activities that keep you away from the truth of God's holy Word? Are you wasting time seeking things that bring so-called fun and temporary satisfaction but don't tear down the walls of limitations in your life? Remember, Jesus said in John 8:31–32 that you must continue in His Word to be His disciple and that the truth you know *and practice* will make you free. It's a choice you make—one that requires diligence and self-discipline. And the choice you make could mean the difference between your living within walls of limitations and lack or breaking out into your destiny!

In our opening text, Gideon was so used to the walls around his life that he had trouble accepting what the angel told him. He couldn't see it; he couldn't picture it. In short, he had trouble with his "vision."

How you see yourself is how you are—your thoughts picture who you are, and you live out those thoughts. (See Proverbs 23:7.) Whose thoughts are you taking? Whose word do you believe? Don't be like Israel in Numbers 13–14 and fail to see yourself the way the faith-filled Word spoken over you says. The Israelites rejected the word of their shepherd and "visionary" and let the resulting walls of limitations cause them to become fearful grasshoppers who got cut off and disinherited from their true destiny and prosperity.

When things get tight and things get tough, you must rely on the spoken word that is given to you. You must keep a vision in your mind of what that word says; you cannot afford to become a victim of what things look like or seem to be on the outside. You must *"walk by faith, not by sight"* (2 Corinthians 5:7).

This is God's mighty hour of the prophetic fulfillment of visions, dreams, and destinies. Now, I have a hint for you: If you tie in wholeheartedly to someone else's godly vision, God will supernaturally expand yours so you can help meet the needs of the one you support. Helping fulfill someone else's dream can empower you to tear down the walls of limitations in your own life.

In fact, God often seems to raise up some individual dispensationally and empower him with a supernatural vision that will enable many of His impoverished people to rise up and tear down the walls of limitations in their lives. In this case, the vision is actually not for the visionary but for the people who are struggling in the confinement of their limitations. Read the book of Nehemiah and see how God used Nehemiah in this way. David did the same thing in 1 Samuel 22:1–2. And even when David encountered Goliath, he did not allow walls of limitations to prevent him from rising up and fulfilling his true destiny!

Tearing down these walls is a mental battle. It's coming against the thoughts planted by the enemy and replacing them with the truth of God's Word. As with anything else regarding such spiritual warfare, there are some obstacles that can prevent you from tearing down the walls of limitations in your life. Look at these carefully, and make a decision not to let a single thing prevent you from fulfilling God's plan for your life!

Obstacles That Prevent You from Tearing Down Walls

1. Slothfulness, laziness, and lack of initiative and diligence on your part. (See Proverbs 6:6–11; 10:4–5; 13:4; 24:30–34.)

2. Disorganization and lack of planning, order, and self-discipline. Does the money you have get dispersed with no written budget, or do you use it to further your vision for your life? Your answer could explain why there's lack and limited finances in your life. (See 1 Corinthians 14:40; Romans 12:11; Luke 16:10–11.)

3. Lack of godly wisdom, which actually comes from godly instruction, chastening, and correction. (See Proverbs 3:11–24; 8:10–21; Hebrews 12:5–11.)

4. Disobedience to God's anointed, taught, and preached Word. How obedient are you to God's Word, spoken from the lips of His shepherds? Many people's poverty and limitations are the result of continual disobedience. Continual obedience, on the other hand, promises prosperity. (See Deuteronomy 11:13–28, chapter 28, 29:9, chapter 30; Job 36:10–12.)

There is a key ingredient in tearing down the walls of limitations in our lives that perhaps you've picked up on in our discussion so far: our faith. Many of us don't realize how much we are capable of having, doing, and experiencing if we would just let our faith work. Romans 12:3 says that God has *"dealt to every man the measure of faith."* But in order for our faith to benefit us, it must have a task, a job, an assignment to remain active and accomplish what it is designed to do.

Let's get into some real Bible study here and take an in-depth look at faith.

> *Even so faith, if it hath not works, is dead, being alone. Yea, a man may say, Thou hast faith, and I have works: show me thy faith without thy works, and I will show thee my faith by my works.* (James 2:17–18)

These verses clearly point out that one's faith can't be seen without a specific job, work, or action to prove that it is alive. You can't get a miracle with dead faith. In fact, without faith you can't even be saved. If your faith is dead, it can't heal you or deliver you. Nothing happens with dead faith. Confess the Word! Then go talk to somebody about what you need, whether it's the car dealer or the mortgage company. In other words, first you tell God what you want to do. "God, I need rent money this month, in Jesus' name." Then God will tell you to use your faith to confess Philippians 4:19: *"My God shall supply all* [my] *need according to his riches in glory by Christ Jesus."* Don't let your faith be lazy. If your faith doesn't have a specific assignment, it is dead. If your faith is dead, it can't keep you healed, and it won't make your marriage work.

These verses also say that faith can be *seen.* There's a Gospel account that bears this out:

> *And again he entered into Capernaum after some days; and it was noised that he was in the house. And*

> *straightway many were gathered together, insomuch that there was no room to receive them, no, not so much as about the door: and he preached the word unto them. And they come unto him, bringing one sick of the palsy, which was borne of four. And when they could not come nigh unto him for the press, they uncovered the roof where he was: and when they had broken it up, they let down the bed wherein the sick of the palsy lay. When Jesus saw their faith, he said unto the sick of the palsy, Son, thy sins be forgiven thee.* (Mark 2:1–5)

These four men gave their faith the job of getting their friend to Jesus, but they did not stop there. When they could not get into the building because of the crowd, they ripped off the roof and let down the bed. Then the passage says, *"When Jesus **saw their faith**, he said unto the sick of the palsy, Son, thy sins be forgiven thee"* (emphasis added). Jesus would not have seen their faith if they had not removed the roof and lowered the man down. This Scripture also shows us that we need to have a second and even a third job for our faith! The first job for these men's faith was to get to the meeting; but because of the crowd, they gave their faith a second job—to get to Jesus, which meant they had to rip off the homeowner's roof! If they had stopped at their first attempt, they would never have gotten their miracle. Jesus saw their faith because it had a job, it was working, and He responded to their efforts. He will respond to our faith as well, as long as it is employed and actively doing its work.

Let's go back to James for another example.

> *Was not Abraham our father justified by works, when he had offered Isaac his son upon the altar? Seest thou how faith wrought with his works, and by works was faith made perfect? And the scripture was fulfilled which*

saith, Abraham believed God, and it was imputed unto him for righteousness: and he was called the Friend of God. (James 2:21–23)

Abraham is considered to be the father of our faith, and even he gave his faith a job. He raised the knife to kill his son Isaac, the son of promise, even though God said his descendants would be as the stars of the sky and the sand on the shore. Hebrews 11, the great chapter on faith, reveals what Abraham's faith was doing: Abraham was willing to kill Isaac because he believed that God would raise him from the dead.

By faith Abraham, when he was tried, offered up Isaac: and he that had received the promises offered up his only begotten son. Of whom it was said, That in Isaac shall thy seed be called: accounting that God was able to raise him up, even from the dead; from whence also he received him in a figure. (Hebrews 11:17–19)

In the end, Abraham did not have to kill Isaac; God had a ram in the bush nearby for the sacrifice. God can provide a ram in the bush for us and move mightily on our behalf, as well, if we will not only live by faith but act by faith. If we will renew our minds to the truth of God's Word and act on it, we will tear down every wall of limitation in our lives.

Ye see then how that by works a man is justified, and not by faith only. (James 2:24)

The word *"works"* in this verse comes from the Greek word *ergon*. Strong's defines *ergon* as "an effort or occupation" and "deed...labour, work."[1]

For as the body without the spirit is dead, so faith without works is dead also. (James 2:26)

♘ All You Need Is a Good Brainwashing

It seems very clear from these verses that if you want the full benefits of miracles, deliverance, and accomplishments in your life and in the lives of others, you'll have to use your faith to tear down the walls of limitations. That means you need to renew your mind to the truth in God's Word, for *"faith cometh by hearing, and hearing by the word of God"* (Romans 10:17).

You'll need to employ your faith to work for your success and your victory in all the endeavors and challenges you face in life. Your faith should work for you toward your inheritance of all the promises of God. That is why it was given to you.

Let's look at Matthew 14:24–25 to find several important things that can motivate us to get our faith off the unemployment line and into a job.

> *But the ship was now in the midst of the sea, tossed with waves: for the wind was contrary.* (v. 24)

Right now you may be in the midst of a wavy sea in your life, a storm in your marriage, a strong wind in your career, a rocking in your finances, and a sinking feeling in your physical or emotional health. If so, it's time to give your faith a job!

> *And in the fourth watch of the night Jesus went unto them, walking on the sea.* (v. 25)

The fourth hour of the night, according to the New English Translation of the Bible, is between the hours of 3:00 and 6:00 a.m., which is usually the darkest point before daybreak. Does this sound like your situation? Is it at its darkest point? If so, get ready for daybreak. It's time for your miracle. There is plenty for your faith to do. Hire your faith to confess the Word of God more, to study more, to meditate more. Hire your faith to forgive. Hire it to move you out. This is not the time to stay in the boat. Your miracle is out there on that wave-tossed water. Out there where things look impossible is where your faith will work the best. Get your faith moving, confess the Word, and watch those walls of limitations come tumbling down!

At the same time, don't forget to hire your faith to pray and fast more. Some things just won't come out of your life without prayer and fasting.

> *If ye have faith as a grain of mustard seed, ye shall say unto this mountain, Remove hence to yonder place; and it shall remove; and nothing shall be impossible unto you. Howbeit this kind goeth not out but by prayer and fasting.* (Matthew 17:20–21)

Prayer, fasting, studying the Word, meditating on the Word, and confessing the Word are ways to employ your faith. Keep in mind that not only is prayer an act of faith, but it also builds faith. Jude 20 talks about *"building up yourselves on your most holy faith, praying in the Holy Ghost."* Prayer will work to get rid of doubt and replace unbelief with belief. Belief is crucial because Jesus said in Mark 9:23, *"All things are possible to him that believeth."*

Now let's look at Peter putting his faith to work in Matthew 14. When we left this scene, the boat was being tossed in the waves.

> *But straightway Jesus spake unto them, saying, Be of good cheer; it is I; be not afraid. And Peter answered him and said, Lord, if it be thou, bid me come unto thee*

51

> *on the water. And he said, Come. And when Peter was*
> *come down out of the ship, he walked on the water, to*
> *go to Jesus.*   (Matthew 14:27–29)

It's important to note here that it was Peter who initiated the challenge. He gave his faith a job. Peter was determined that his faith would not stay lazy and die. He gave his faith what we would consider to be an impossible job— except that Matthew 17:20 and Mark 9:23 say that nothing is impossible. If we just look to Jesus, the Author and the Finisher of our faith, we can give our faith any job within God's will, and it will work.

Once you get your faith off the unemployment line—out of the boat of fear, doubt, hopelessness, and despair—and give it a specific job, you'll find out just how much God wants to do in your life. And even if you begin to sink while doing the work your faith gets you into, Jesus will catch you like He caught Peter and keep you from failing. He won't let you be destroyed.

> *But when* [Peter] *saw the wind boisterous, he was*
> *afraid; and beginning to sink, he cried, saying, Lord, save*
> *me. And immediately Jesus stretched forth his hand,*
> *and caught him, and said unto him, O thou of little faith,*
> *wherefore didst thou doubt? And when they were come*
> *into the ship, the wind ceased.*   (Matthew 14:30–32)

Things may look dark in your situation, but the dawn will come. Some of you are just one effort away from your miracle. What is in your mind right now? What thoughts are winning the battle in your mind? When the disciples saw Jesus walking on the water, they thought He was a ghost. Why do people always imagine the worst? Even if you believe, your faith alone will not accomplish what you need—you need to do something regarding what you believe.

Peter created an assignment for his faith. He looked out beyond the walls of limitations. Don't be afraid to give your faith a job that you have never done before. Don't be afraid to give your faith a job that you have never seen anyone else do before. James 2:22 says that faith is made perfect by works. All your faith needs is a job, and it won't go wrong. If you follow it, it can make your life a success; it can heal your body, help your marriage, and make you prosperous. It will tear down the walls of limitations in your life!

Let me mention one other thing. Note that Peter asked Jesus to tell him to do something. He said, *"Lord, if it be thou, bid me come unto thee on the water"* (Matthew 14:28). Job 36:11 says that the rewards for obedience are *"days in prosperity, and...years in pleasures."* Try something that will require you to obey God. When they were in the boat, the disciples were afraid. You're not called to be afraid; you're called to step out.

It may be the darkest hour of your storm. Every part of your life depends on your faith working, so don't look too hard at your situation. Don't look at the height of the walls limiting you. Peter did not have any trouble walking on the water until he took his eyes off Jesus and looked at where he was. Remember, *"we walk by faith, not by sight"* (2 Corinthians 5:7). *"The just shall live by faith"* (Hebrews 10:38). God won't let you die on the water. Peter began to sink because of fear, but Jesus was right there to keep him from failing.

Give your faith the job to ask and to think and to tear down the walls of limitations in your life. God is so much bigger than even our asking and thinking! "[God] *is able to do exceeding abundantly above all that we ask or think, according to the power that worketh in us*" (Ephesians 3:20). He wants much more for us than the failures we see. God wants more for us than even the success we have already seen. Tear down those walls! His Word declares His truth: He wants us to know Him better. He wants us to be healed. He wants our marriages to be blessed. He wants us to be prosperous and to abound in good works. Release your faith. God is able. Break the chains around your heart. Tear down the walls surrounding your mind. All things are possible to those who believe. Fight the good fight of faith. God has given you the victory through your Lord and Savior Jesus Christ. There is plenty for your faith to do. Let it work, and watch your miracle come to pass.

Notes

[1] James Strong, *Strong's Hebrew and Greek Dictionaries* (Cedar Rapids, Iowa: Parsons Technology, Inc., Electronic Edition STEP Files © 1998), #G2041.

4

Removing Stumbling Blocks That Prevent Your Destiny

4

Removing Stumbling Blocks That Prevent Your Destiny

You have a destiny, and that destiny is related to God's prophecy, to what He has written and spoken in His Word. The devil knows this, so he tries to thwart God's destiny for you by infiltrating your mind. The powers of darkness will hover over your life, accusing you and trying to find your weaknesses or cracks in your spiritual armor, so that they can cause you to think thoughts contrary to God's will and the fulfillment of His destiny for you. Therefore, how you process God's Word and live your life—how you fight this battle against the enemy—is directly tied to what God has declared in His Word as belonging to you and as part of your destiny.

All you need is a good brainwashing—you need to change your mind to what the Word of God says. *"For as* [a man] *thinketh in his heart, so is he"* (Proverbs 23:7). When you start thinking outside of what God's Word says about you, when you believe whatever thoughts the enemy feeds you, when you start confessing things that are different from what God says about you—you are automatically putting yourself in a position in which God's promises cannot be fulfilled and your God-given destiny is aborted.

God wants to fulfill what He has declared is your destiny. At the same time, the principalities and rulers of darkness and spiritual wickedness in high places are going to be doing everything they can to thwart it. They are going to be throwing stumbling blocks into your path every chance they get.

No matter what situation you find yourself in today, let it be known that God wants you to prosper and has ordained you to have an abundant life. Before the foundation of the world, God chose you and predestined you to be adopted as His child through the shed blood of Jesus Christ. (See Ephesians 1:4–5.) This is God's intention for you. God's plans are those that will allow you to prosper in every way, exceeding abundantly above all that you can ask or think. That is the truth, an irrefutable fact. But how and if you prosper is up to you. Yes, you prosper according to the power that God has already given to work within you (Ephesians 3:20). But it is up to you whether you limit that power or allow that power free exercise. It all goes back to the battle in the mind and what you know and believe.

Second Peter 1:3 says that God's *"divine power hath given unto us all things that pertain unto life and godliness, through the knowledge of him that hath called us to glory and virtue."* It is through the knowledge of God that we are able to obtain these things. Hosea 4:6 says, *"My people are destroyed for lack of knowledge."* God has already given you the power to enable you to fulfill your destiny, but you need to know what it is and how to use it in order for it to work for you.

Jesus told us in Luke 10:19, *"Behold, I give unto you power to tread on serpents and scorpions, and over all the power of the enemy: and nothing shall by any means hurt you."* The devil knows that God has given you this power over him! (Actually, these words of Jesus are a fulfillment of the prophecy in Genesis 3:15, which Satan surely remembered down through the ages.) You need to realize that the devil will stop at nothing to keep you from using your delegated power and authority to accomplish God's plans and purposes for your life. And one of his main tactics is to make you think that your present situation is your permanent destination; he wants you to feel frustrated, hopeless, and alone.

The devil is a liar and a thief who came only to steal, kill, and destroy. However, Jesus came that we might have life— and have it more abundantly. (See John 10:10.) The words *"more abundantly"* in the Scripture come from the Greek word *perissos,* which means "beyond; superabundant...exceeding abundantly above...beyond measure."[1] This means that no matter how smart you are, how rich you are, or even how satisfied you are, your destiny is beyond where you are right now. You see, God's thoughts are never centered on your problems because He doesn't see you with a problem or in a negative situation. He already sees you beyond where you think you are. He sees you in your fulfilled destiny!

Quite often we get discouraged because we don't understand that God has empowered us with supernatural strength not just to endure, but to overcome. Because we haven't grasped this, we often fall back on or use our weaknesses, problems, or faults to make excuses for not fulfilling our God-given destiny. Let me give you some advice. If you feel weak and your situation seems hopeless, don't just say so! The Word says in Joel 3:10, *"Let the weak say, I am strong."* If you say what the enemy has presented to you, he wins. If you say what God says in His Word, then you win! Whenever you speak words that are in agreement with your problem, your weakness, or your lack, instead of words that God has prophesied regarding His profitable plans for you, then you are speaking idle words and laying down a stumbling block for your downfall and condemnation. (See Matthew 12:36–37.) To put it another way, your thoughts establish your circumstances. Whatever you think and speak becomes effective in your life. *"A man shall be satisfied with good by the fruit of his mouth"* (Proverbs 12:14)—conversely, his life will be filled with problems if the fruit of his mouth is contrary to God's thoughts!

You need to get your thoughts in alignment with God's thoughts for you. You need to say what He says. Why? What He says gets accomplished. *"So shall my word be that goeth forth out of my mouth: it shall not return unto me void, but it shall accomplish that which I please, and it shall prosper in the thing whereto I sent it"* (Isaiah 55:11). If you keep your words aligned with the Word of God, He is obligated to perform anything in your life relative to His Word. God *"will hasten [His] word to perform it"* (Jeremiah 1:12), but you must speak the Word of God in order for that word to be hastened toward its manifestation in your life.

Whatever God says He will do for you, He will do. Psalm 89:34 says, *"My covenant will I not break, nor alter the thing that is gone out of my lips."* The plans that God has for you have already been prophesied throughout all sixty-six books of the Bible. But if you don't read the Word of God, you can't know the Word of God. And if you don't know the Word of

God, you can't speak the Word of God. If you don't speak the Word of God, then out of ignorance you will speak words that destroy God's will for your destiny. And that leads you to the stumbling blocks that the enemy so subtly and not-so-subtly uses to derail your destiny.

These stumbling blocks are related to varying degrees of attitudes, but all are rooted in the heart. They also may start off rather innocuously, but the devil has a way of escalating the damage. By the time a person has reached the depths of these things, he has some serious issues to deal with and repent of.

Ignorance

Ignorance is one of the most subtle stumbling blocks because it keeps people from realizing or correcting the other ones. Again, knowledge is the key in this mental battle, and ignorance is diametrically opposed to learning and gaining wisdom. Ephesians 4:18 tells us that ignorance and blindness of heart alienate us from the life of God and all its riches. God's intention, on the other hand, is for us to increase in knowledge so that we may fulfill our destiny.

Low Self-Esteem

God created us, so He knows the quality of our characters, our capabilities, and our potentials. Unfortunately, people quite often deny God's ability and lay stumbling blocks for themselves because they have low self-esteem or a poor self-image. We need to renew our minds to the truth: The work of God is always superior, not inferior. David praised God for his own self-worth in Psalm 139:14 where he said, *"I will praise thee; for I am fearfully and wonderfully made: marvellous are thy works; and that my soul knoweth right well."* He wasn't boasting or being proud; he was simply acknowledging the good that God had created in him.

Numbers 13:17–33 provide us with another example of good self-esteem versus a poor self-image. Ten of the twelve men Moses sent to spy in the Promised Land brought back an evil report: They saw themselves as losers instead of the winners that God saw them as. Only Caleb and Joshua brought back a good report by saying, *"Let us go up at once, and possess* [the land]; *for we are well able to overcome it"* (v. 30). Caleb and Joshua could say this so positively because they knew their God. In Daniel 11:32 the Scripture says, *"The people that do know their God shall be strong, and do exploits."* The truth is, you can have the confidence in God in you!

Laziness

Laziness, or slothfulness, is a stumbling block because it prevents you from wholeheartedly pursuing God. When we should be seeking to do and learn all that we can, laziness will cause us to find excuses not to do anything. Proverbs 6:9–11 tells us that laziness sets the stage for poverty, while Proverbs 13:4 goes on to say that even though the soul of the slothful may desire things, he will not obtain them. Instead, it is the desires of the soul of the diligent that will be satisfied. If we make the sincere effort to overcome laziness by forcing ourselves to be diligent in prayer and fasting as it says in Isaiah 58:6–12, the yokes of bondage will be destroyed in our lives and our souls will be satisfied without lack.

Mediocrity

Mediocrity is a direct result of laziness and slothfulness. This stumbling block often exists in the lives of God's people

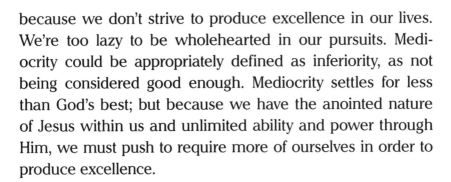
because we don't strive to produce excellence in our lives. We're too lazy to be wholehearted in our pursuits. Mediocrity could be appropriately defined as inferiority, as not being considered good enough. Mediocrity settles for less than God's best; but because we have the anointed nature of Jesus within us and unlimited ability and power through Him, we must push to require more of ourselves in order to produce excellence.

We have been created in the image of God and strengthened with all might according to His glorious power to do the work of God. Because the nature of God is excellent, the work of our hands must be excellent as well. Colossians 3:23–24 teaches us that whatever we do, we should do it heartily as to the Lord and not to men. This, in turn, will lead to our receiving favor from both God and man. When we turn away from mediocrity and begin to pursue excellence in our prayer and fasting, praise and worship, Bible study, and holy living, the results are manifested in prosperity at every level and in every facet of our lives, including relationships, finances, and careers. However, achieving excellence requires diligence; therefore, we must not allow laziness and mediocrity to cause us to miss our blessings.

Disobedience

More than just a stumbling block, disobedience is downright sin. God desires for us to know Him in the intimacy of His fellowship, but it is always our choice to obey or disobey. In Isaiah 1:18–19 He said, *"Come now, and let us reason together...though your sins be as scarlet, they shall be as white as snow; though they be red like crimson, they shall be as wool. If ye be willing and obedient, ye shall eat the good of the land."* The Word of God says in Deuteronomy 11:26–28, *"Behold, I set before you this day a blessing and a curse; a blessing, if ye obey the commandments of the LORD your God, which I command you this day: and a curse, if ye will not obey the commandments of the LORD your God."* God makes it clear that the choice to obey Him is ours alone. No one else can make this choice for us or take this choice from us.

Pride/Anger

The next two types of stumbling blocks are the most difficult ones to eradicate. Pride, anger, and intolerance are often the cement that holds the next stumbling blocks together. Unfortunately, when we justify all our other stumbling blocks with pride or anger, the enemy can easily slip us into the deep pit of unforgiveness and bitterness.

Unforgiveness/Bitterness

Together, pride, anger, intolerance, hate, unforgiveness, and bitterness block the divine flow of the anointing we need to thrust us out from our limited past and into our supernatural future and destiny. They also prevent divine love from flowing into our lives, which in turn hinders our faith and confidence in God to work in our situation and the fulfillment of our destiny. Mark 11:25–26 teaches us that God will not receive our prayers if we harbor unforgiveness in our hearts. Why? If we cannot forgive others of the trespasses they have made against us, then God will not forgive us of the trespasses we have made against Him. This is a very sobering truth.

What qualities should we, the elect of God, have instead of unforgiveness and bitterness? Colossians 3:12–13 lists them for us: *"bowels of mercies, kindness, humbleness of mind, meekness, longsuffering; forbearing one another, and forgiving one another, if any man have a quarrel against any: even as Christ forgave you, so also do ye."*

Everything that we have and can become is because of God's unrelenting and eternal love for us. It is only as we return His love by keeping His commandments through the knowledge of His Word and the power of His Spirit that we can remove every stumbling block that prevents us from reaching our destiny.

Failure to remove these stumbling blocks can result in things like poverty and failure. Poverty is not a blessing. Failure is not a blessing. These things are results of being cursed. Now, poverty is hard to define. Poverty does not necessarily mean you lack material necessities. You can have a lot of things and still be poor. You might have three cars in your garage, but you also might have three high payments to go with them. Some families spend half of their income on car payments! That's not blessing. That's not prosperity. You might have a nice big house, but if you struggle with your mortgage, you're in poverty. You might have a suit for every Sunday in the month, plus one in case there is a fifth Sunday, but if you paid for them with a credit card you have charged to the limit, that is not prosperity. The blessings of God would include your coming out of debt and not getting back into it!

Let's take a look at how stumbling blocks trip us up in everyday life. Let's start with something small. What if no one had taken the time to teach you how to tie your shoes? Wouldn't that be a shame? Here you are, a grown adult, and unable to tie your own shoes. You wouldn't be living up to your potential with no shoes.

○ All You Need Is a Good Brainwashing

I remember dealing with a young man in our academy some time ago. We have a rule for our athletes that, when they travel, the young men are required to wear a necktie. This young man rarely wore the required tie. Everyone thought he was trying to be difficult and arrogant, but I sensed something different. I pulled him aside one day and questioned him. Do you know what I found out? He had never learned how to tie a necktie. His mother had often tied it for him, but she had never taught him how to tie it himself.

There are a lot of things I wish I had found out a long time ago. Ignorance is the basic stumbling block that acts as the foundation for many of the others. I have learned things about the world's financial system that, had I known them years earlier, would have made me much more prosperous than I am now. Ignorance kept me from reaching my potential.

In Matthew 25, Jesus told the parable of the talents. To one servant the man gave five talents, to another he gave two, and to another he gave one. The one who received five talents invested them and earned five more. The servant who received two talents invested them and earned two more. Those are one hundred percent returns. (One of the things I've learned is that there are places today where investments can yield a hundred percent return!) However, the servant who had been given one talent took it and buried it in the ground. Do you know what Jesus called that servant? Wicked and slothful! Remember, the story says that the man gave to each servant *"according to his...ability."* So this last servant had capabilities but didn't use them.

We cannot afford to be ignorant. We have to be willing to learn, and then once we learn something, we can't be lazy.

For instance, if you had $10,000, $50,000, or even $500,000, would you know what to do with it? You have to acquire some knowledge. The world system today, for the most part, is set up so that the average man will continue to struggle just to have very little. Such a continuous struggle does not do very much for one's self-esteem. A low self-esteem or poor self-image will keep you in lack, keep you deficient, and keep you operating in mediocrity. Do you know what? God has more for you! Turn those stumbling blocks into stepping-stones.

So many of us have been deceived into thinking that the best we can do is live from paycheck to paycheck, hand-to-mouth. We think we're supposed to struggle with what little we have. Let me give you some advice. Anything that eats up your time, drains your precious energy, gives you gray hairs, and still does not produce anything is not worth your time! Don't waste time spinning your wheels and not moving; change your mind and strive for excellence. Reach for your potential!

Don't be unwilling to change. If God's Word says one thing and you're doing another, then change! Don't stay in the problem. Romans 12:11 says, "[Be] *not slothful in business."* Some of us, rather than apply some diligence and work, want to stay in pride and hang on to the problem. I have gone through times in my walk with God where I had to change just about everything I thought I was doing right because I was doing it my way and not God's way. I haven't regretted making those changes—obedience brings blessing, but disobedience is a stumbling block!

Sometimes we fail to listen and obey the right things. Deuteronomy 28:1–14 talks about the blessings of God. But don't skip verse 1: *"If thou shalt hearken diligently unto the voice of the Lord thy God, to observe and to do all his commandments which I command thee this day."* Disobedience blocks the blessings of God. We've mentioned the following Scripture before, but it bears repeating:

> *He openeth also their ear to discipline, and commandeth that they return from iniquity. If they obey and serve him, they shall spend their days in prosperity, and their years in pleasures. But if they obey not, they shall perish by the sword, and they shall die without knowledge.*
> (Job 36:10–12)

I don't know about you, but *"days in prosperity"* and *"years in pleasures"* sound a lot better than death by the sword! Now, that can be translated into death by high mortgages, death by high interest rates, death by outrageous debt, death by overdue bills, death by marital friction, or death by bankruptcy. It's all deadly. In fact, these things are causes of stress, and it is well documented that stress is a cause of many serious illnesses. We have to seek God for wisdom and take Him at His Word.

His Word says we are blessed. Now, we know that we are saved by grace and covered by the blood of Jesus, but when we say we are blessed, do we really know what that means? I'm not saying that we are not blessed, but we need to look at ourselves and look at the Bible and see if we really have God's blessings in our lives. We have to be able to compare our lives to the Word of God and remove anything in the way of really having what God wants us to have. We have to challenge ourselves. There is no failure in God. If our business is under God, it may struggle briefly because we are human, but it won't fail. If our career is under God and we are of

God, every day may not be sunshine, but we won't fail in our career. If we're blessed in our career and in our business, whoever is involved with us also will be blessed. That's scriptural—in Genesis 39 Joseph was blessed, and everything he touched was blessed. As a result, everything Potiphar owned prospered because of Joseph. If we are blessed, then whatever we touch and whatever we do should be blessed. We all should want to be that effective. So we need to examine ourselves and our activities and see if we are as effective as we should be (2 Corinthians 13:5).

Joseph wasn't supposed to be a slave. His own brothers sold him into slavery just to get rid of him. It looked like he was cursed, but because Joseph was blessed, even a stumbling block like being a slave couldn't keep him down. People can put stumbling blocks in your way. Someone can even go as far as to curse your life, but righteousness can remove every obstacle. Being faithful to God, as Joseph was, will override every situation. The circumstances may try to surround you, but the righteousness inside you will remove every stumbling block, and you will still come out on top.

Even when things come to knock you down, you'll be able to get up. Failure does not come from getting knocked down; it comes from staying down. You work so hard for your money, but it seems like you never get ahead. Don't stay down; get on God's plan and make your money work for you. Let me give you an example.

When you get your refund at tax time, instead of debt consolidation, as we have known it, consider something I like to call "self-consolidation." That is where you take part of your tax refund and eliminate part of your debt. You can start with the bill that has the least amount of time left until it will be paid in full. Suppose you have a balance of $4,000, and your payment is $200 per month for the next twenty months. If you pay that $4,000 debt with your refund, then you have $200 extra each month. Instead of spending that money, apply it to the principal of another debt—preferably the one with the next shortest time left in its amortization period. A $3,000 debt with thirty months left paying $100 a month would be a prime candidate. Pay an extra $200 each month toward that debt, and instead of taking thirty months to pay this debt, it will take only ten months. Now, in ten short months, you have given yourself an extra $300 each month to attack your remaining debt.

Let's take it one step further. You may have a payment of $300 a month for a $12,000 debt. It should take forty more months to pay, but here you have an extra $300 per month because you consolidated your own debt. Adding this extra $300 to your monthly payment will cut your time in half. Before you know it, in less than three years, you will have gotten rid of $19,000 of debt. Instead of going to the lender or getting a second job, you have created spendable income by eliminating your debt. This is a simple scenario, and it doesn't even consider the effect of extra payments on debts that are calculated with interest—like a mortgage.

For most mortgages, the first ten years is all interest. If you pay your mortgage every month for thirty years, you will have paid for your home three and a half times. Yes, Proverbs 22:7 is true: *"The borrower is servant to the lender."* Friend, you did not buy three houses; you only bought one, so why pay for it three times? Just sending $100 extra for your mortgage in a separate check applied directly to the principal will cut, on average, ten years off the term of the loan. In fact, just making a payment at closing will cut off an additional five years. We get so spiritual. When I prepared to purchase a home, I would pray, "Lord, please let them only want five percent down instead of ten percent." In reality, I was praying for more debt. I should have been praying, "Lord, prosper me so that I can put twenty percent down, or better yet, multiply me so that I can just buy a house with cash." The supernatural blessings of God would have you own your home with no payment. The supernatural blessings of God would have you burning your mortgage papers in ten years or less, instead of thirty. Let's not be ignorant. We need to get more wisdom.

Remember, each stumbling block can lead to another one. If you trip over the stumbling block of ignorance and don't know much, you most likely will have low self-esteem. If you have a poor self-image, you are bound to be slothful and lazy. These, in turn, will cause you to operate in mediocrity instead of excellence. Living in mediocrity will create a comfort zone that can breed stubbornness and an unwillingness to change. And that can lead you into bitterness against anyone who tries to help you! Your pastor could speak a word that would turn your situation around and bring you out. But if, with all these stumbling blocks in the way, you refuse to heed the law of truth that can make you free from your problem, then you will hold on in stubbornness, comfortable in your lack. It will pacify you and crucify you at the same time. You'd rather keep pulling your little red wagon while all the time God wants you to have a ten-ton truck.

If only we would just listen, apply, and obey the Word of God! Instead we struggle to stay alive. We struggle to stay married. We struggle with debt. We struggle with bad health.

ॐ All You Need Is a Good Brainwashing

We struggle with parenting and, in our "spirituality," call it the glory of God. That is not truth! Proverbs 10:22 says, *"The blessing of the LORD, it maketh rich, and he addeth no sorrow with it."*

Which will we choose? The truth or the enemy's lies? Proverbs 12:28 says that there is no death in the way of righteousness; yet we tend to struggle just to stay alive. We struggle to stay married, while all the time the Scripture says, *"Marriage is honourable in all, and the bed undefiled"* (Hebrews 13:4) and "[Submit] *yourselves one to another in the fear of God"* (Ephesians 5:21). Deuteronomy 28:12 says we are to lend to nations and not borrow, but we struggle with debt. We deal with bad health instead of believing Exodus 23:25, in which God says, *"I will take sickness away from the midst of thee."* We struggle with parenting rather than believing Proverbs 22:6: *"Train up a child in the way he should go: and when he is old, he will not depart from it."*

The Word is the only thing that will remedy the problems you face. All you need is a good brainwashing. When you know the truth and act on that truth, it will set you free. (See John 8:32.) God's Word maps out your destiny of blessing, victory, and success. So check your life; examine your thoughts. What stumbling blocks has the devil put in your way? Tear them down with the truth of the holy Word of God. Don't be ignorant!

> *Blessed be the Lord, who daily loadeth us with benefits, even the God of our salvation.* (Psalm 68:19)

> *God, who giveth us richly all things to enjoy.* (1 Timothy 6:17)

Notes

[1] James Strong, *Strong's Hebrew and Greek Dictionaries* (Cedar Rapids, Iowa: Parsons Technology, Inc., Electronic Edition STEP Files © 1998), #G4053.

5

Get a Grip on Your Mind and Get a Grip on Your Life

5

Get a Grip on Your Mind and Get a Grip on Your Life

It's a known fact that you become what you think. Proverbs 23:7 says, *"For as* [a man] *thinketh in his heart, so is he."* A wild, uncontrolled mind produces a wild, uncontrolled life. Conversely, a wild, uncontrolled life reveals that your mind is running wild and out of control. Is your mind loose, out of control, and out of touch with the truth of God's Word about you? When is the last time you really got a good, solid grip on your thought processes?

Both Peter and Paul gave some very clear instructions that will help you get a grip on your mind and get a grip on your life.

> *Wherefore gird up the loins of your mind, be sober, and hope to the end for the grace that is to be brought unto you at the revelation of Jesus Christ.* (1 Peter 1:13)

> *Finally, brethren, whatsoever things are true, whatsoever things are honest, whatsoever things are just,*

whatsoever things are pure, whatsoever things are lovely, whatsoever things are of good report; if there be any virtue, and if there be any praise, think on these things. (Philippians 4:8)

These two verses clearly show us that we have the ability to get a grip on our minds and on our lives. They tell us that we are the wardens and gatekeepers of our own minds. We're the ones who decide what enters our minds. If we allow continual thoughts of depression, worry, fear, doubt, anxiety, negativity, and fear, then we open the door to our own failure, and sometimes even disaster.

Take David, for example. He had an opportunity to let discouragement and despair overtake his mind, but he didn't. Instead, he turned to the Spirit of God and filled his mind with God's thoughts rather than with what the circumstances looked like.

And David was greatly distressed; for the people spake of stoning him, because the soul of all the people was grieved, every man for his sons and for his daughters: but David encouraged himself in the LORD his God. (1 Samuel 30:6)

What kind of life do you want? If you want to experience the continual blessings, prosperity, and victory that God has ordained for you, then you need to monitor the thoughts you think. You need to grab hold of your thought patterns and tune in to the Holy Spirit. You need to let the Word of God get a good grip on your mind, which has been running wild and loose in doubt, fear, worry, and other negativity.

Look closely at what Paul said in 1 Corinthians 2:9–10:

*But as it is written, Eye hath not seen, nor ear heard,
neither have entered into the heart of man, the things
which God hath prepared for them that love him. But
God hath revealed them unto us by his Spirit: for the
Spirit searcheth all things, yea, the deep things of God.*

Once you let the Word grab hold of your thought patterns
and you tune in to the Holy Spirit, your mind will begin to
tune out the negative things that are destroying your faith and
start processing the supernaturally powerful things that God's
thoughts are to you. Before you know it, you'll be empowered
and will start seeking His face with great expectation. Your
thoughts will become His thoughts and your ways His ways.
As John 14:12 says, you'll begin to believe and do the works
Jesus did: *"Verily, verily, I say unto you, He that believeth on
me, the works that I do shall he do also; and greater works
than these shall he do; because I go unto my Father."*

We have the mind of Christ. (See 1 Corinthians 2:16.) We
can think God's thoughts concerning us instead of the enemy
proposals, which only suggest failure, sickness, defeat, poverty, weakness, fear, worry, anger, resentment, inferiority, and
many other negative emotions. And we know that what God
has thought and purposed will come to pass!

*The LORD of hosts hath sworn, saying, Surely as I have
thought, so shall it come to pass; and as I have purposed, so shall it stand....For the LORD of hosts hath
purposed, and who shall disannul it? and his hand is
stretched out, and who shall turn it back?*

(Isaiah 14:24, 27)

God has already set His divine thoughts into eternal
motion, and they will stand and come to pass. If you'll just

discipline your thoughts to agree with His prophetic word, you'll get a grip on your mind and your life.

> *So shall my word be that goeth forth out of my mouth: it shall not return unto me void, but it shall accomplish that which I please, and it shall prosper in the thing whereto I sent it. For ye shall go out with joy, and be led forth with peace: the mountains and the hills shall break forth before you into singing, and all the trees of the field shall clap their hands. Instead of the thorn shall come up the fir tree, and instead of the brier shall come up the myrtle tree: and it shall be to the LORD for a name, for an everlasting sign that shall not be cut off.*
> (Isaiah 55:11–13)

Once we get our minds renewed to God's mind and thoughts, then the word He sends to us will be accomplished in us and prosper us. We will go out with supernatural joy and peace, and even the elements of the earth will praise Him, for God delights in fulfilling His prophetic, eternal will and word through our lives.

Again, everything begins in the mind. I cannot emphasize this enough. Right now, whatever is keeping your life unproductive originated in your mind. Actually, certain negative, destructive things in our hearts would never have lodged there if they had not been in our thoughts first. For example, all the emotions that destroy a marriage—such as unforgiveness, distrust, anger, hatred, jealousy, and others—start in the mind. All the things that cause sin and destruction—such as lust, fornication, adultery, deceit, drug and alcohol addiction, perversion, among others—start in the mind. Even poverty is a mentality before it ever becomes a lifestyle.

Get a grip on your mind so you can get a grip on your life! If you want to know what is in your mind, just check out what is coming from your mouth. Jesus taught this very significant principle of truth in Matthew 15:17–20 to help His disciples and us understand that when we fail to get a grip on our minds, we fail to get a grip on our lives and so we become defiled.

> *Do not ye yet understand, that whatsoever entereth in at the mouth goeth into the belly, and is cast out into the draught? But those things which proceed out of the mouth come forth from the heart; and they defile the man. For out of the heart proceed evil thoughts, murders, adulteries, fornications, thefts, false witness, blasphemies: these are the things which defile a man: but to eat with unwashen hands defileth not a man.*

It all comes back to what we think.

At this point, there are a couple of things I want to talk about that will help you get a grip on your mind and thought processes and change your life. The first is "routines and ruts."

There are two kinds of routines—good and bad. Your life is full of routines, some of them good and some of them bad. Bad routines result from losing your grip on the discipline, determination, and energy God gave you. You must have the right routines in your life. A good routine leads to prosperity. When you lose the grip on your mind, you can get stuck in routines that take you from the realm of excellence and transport you back to the realm of mediocrity.

Simply put, bad routines lead to ruts. And sometimes we lose the grip on our lives because we've allowed ourselves to become stuck in ruts. I asked my wife one day if the word *rut* was in the dictionary. I used it so much that I thought it was slang. I looked it up, and my dictionary defined *rut* as a fixed, monotonous, boring routine. If we are honest, we have quite a few of those in our lives. We try to act like our lives are exciting, but we drink out of the same coffee cup and use the same toothbrush we should have replaced four years ago. We are still dealing with socks that are ready to put themselves on our feet, and some of the same "naps" we never combed are still in our hair. We need to take a look at these things!

Just as there are good and bad routines, there are also spiritual and natural routines. So many people want to hit a home run in the spiritual realm, and they can't even get to first base in the natural. We say, "Oh, God, bring me home a millionaire; let me be the best at everything," and we don't even have a natural routine that will lead to prosperity. We want home runs in the spiritual but strike out in the natural.

People in a rut love where they are. They feel satisfied and don't like challenges. They don't like ambitious people coming around them. They mistake a helping hand for a hurting hand. For them, the only way out of the rut is a helping hand, but they are depressed with so much anxiety and fear that when that hand comes, they think someone wants their job. Their jobs have become nothing in their hands, yet they can get too stuck in a rut to ever change, and they have managed to drag everything about their jobs into the rut with them.

Ambitious people, on the other hand, don't want a non-impacting, non-productive, boring job. If you're in a rut, you offend those who are not. Think about it. Nothing is more offensive than a person who is not trying to go anywhere and is in your way, especially when you were the one who put that person there! You know where you're going and what belongs to you, and someone is blocking the road. People who are going somewhere are offended by those who are not, and people who are not going anywhere are offended by those who are. A lot of conflict in the world is between these two kinds of people. It is always about people in the way and people making a way. If you don't want to be in the way, then you'd better make sure you are making a way!

Whatever routine you follow, it should lead to something that is productive. For instance, a good routine would be an appropriate exercise routine. Senior citizens who volunteer and remain active in their bodies remain active in their minds. It's been medically proven that activity will enhance and extend life. (Obviously, the mind is the key, for the first thing to go in old age is the brain cells!) If your routine does not produce prosperity or good fruit, it is a bad routine. What do you do then? Simple: *Change it.* Sometimes you have to make radical changes to get out of your rut.

Let me give you a simple example. For a long time I would go on my daily run in the same tired sweat suit. I always claimed that I didn't have time to get a new one. One day I decided that I was going to get out of that rut. I told my secretary, "Bump everybody today." I was tired of not making it to the bank. That day, I went to the bank, cashed some checks, got some money in my hands, went to the department store, and got a new sweat suit. I determined that I was going to run in something new that was soft and smelled nice. I determined that I was going to break out of that rut.

You are the only one who can get you out of your rut, unless you want someone to give you a push or a kick. The truth is, if you wanted to move, you would have moved. For the most part, people are lazy. We simply ignore our mess. And when people come along to try and move us out of our ruts verbally, we get mad. Well, I'm about to do that to you, so get ready.

I tell our people that they should have a pile of money in the bank by the time they're twenty. I started working by running errands when I was seven years old. I shined shoes, old Stacy Adams biscuit-toed shoes. I had to use bleach and a toothbrush to make them white in the stitches. People didn't want a crayon; they wanted the natural stitch back. If nothing else, you ought to have a car with no note when you're twenty because you started when you were sixteen!

I am trying to force you into success, here. Change your mind and change your life. Don't be so stubborn in your thinking that you don't head for success.

And that leads me to the second thing I want to talk about: excellence.

And this I pray, that your love may abound yet more and more in knowledge and in all judgment; that ye may approve things that are excellent; that ye may be sincere and without offence till the day of Christ; being filled with the fruits of righteousness, which are by Jesus Christ, unto the glory and praise of God.
(Philippians 1:9–11)

Paul wrote this, and Paul was a very spiritual man. He had many revelations and wrote more epistles than any other person. Why would such a spiritual man want to teach about excellence? He knew that people who were supernaturally empowered by the Word of God had to pursue natural excellence.

Some of us say that we are saved and blessed, but dress so mediocre. Others of us say that we are filled with the Spirit of God, but then talk in a sub-par way for people full of the most powerful entity in the universe. When we refuse to strive for excellence, we shortchange who God is. We make Him out to be a God who can only produce people who walk around with a stick and a bag on their backs, jumping on freight cars, going to the mission for a handout, and singing nice Christmas songs. God is hardly ever made out to be One who can produce above-average people who accomplish supernatural feats, who strive for financial dynamos, and who are about excellence in everything they do. We believers have made it look like that excellence has nothing to do with God.

The sad truth is that if you go through corporate America and check through the ranks, you'll find that most of the people spending two hours in the break room are Christians. Most of the ones you find begging, whining, and complaining about how bad it is are the saved folk. Then you might find a man who is mean, cusses all the time, and doesn't look like he has anything of God in him at all, and he is neither broke nor poor. You see, it is not what you say that counts, but what you do.

So many people go into job interviews and do a lot of talking. "I can and I've been and I've done...." Then after the employer hires them, the manager believes those people should have gone to Broadway. "I should have sent them to Hollywood. They missed their call. They could have done real well in a non-reality world."

Look at your life. Look at your productivity. If what is in your life isn't good, don't approve it. If what is in your life isn't good, don't accept it. If what is in your life isn't good, don't get comfortable with it. If what is in your life isn't good, don't get satisfied with it. *Change it.*

I'm a challenger. I want to make you go for success. Get a grip on your mind and get a grip on your life! I understand what corporate success is. I worked successfully before I was saved, so I know very well that now I have to go way beyond where I was while in the world.

I can push you, but it's up to you to change. Decide you won't stop until you get to excellence. Decide you won't stop until you see the best. Anybody can sit around and wait for someone else to either say he is okay or fix what is wrong with his life. But are you willing to grow up enough to fix your own mess? Are you willing to go on trial with yourself every day and change yourself? Look in the mirror and say, "You're not what I want to be; you're what I've got, but I will change you." Decide to change and improve what you see in that mirror. Tell that reflection, every time you see it, that it will look better. Raise your level of thinking. Just knowing where you're at won't help you. You have to do something about it. In one sense, you have to get hungry enough to pay the price.

So you want a new leather jacket. Do you know what that costs? You say you want designer clothes, but have you checked what you'll have to sacrifice? So many people look at what others have and want the same, but they don't check the price. They don't realize what they would have to pay.

To have what these people do, you have to be hungry. A hungry person will hurt you. If you don't believe me, go down a street in the dark with a bone in your hand and meet a hungry person. That bone could be anything you have that he wants— money, food, jewelry. He'll hurt you. Hungry people are desperate, and they won't stop until they get what they want.

Whatever goes on in your life, if it's mediocre, why let it go on? The approval process starts with you. You're the one who has approved a prayer life that can't move a roach. You're the one who has approved a study life that only includes opening the Bible when you go to church. Do what you have to do to change. Do whatever it takes to go for excellence. Use your faith. Set up a schedule, if necessary. You'll never really understand the Word of God like you should if you don't go over it again and again. It is like athletics. In athletics, fundamentals are practiced over and over so that at game time, the players know what to do. Constant repetition is the key. You will learn only as you go back over things. If you are not involved in the "successive, progressive rehearsal of things," you won't be able to carry out what you need to do when the demand comes and the pressure is on you. You need discipline so that something develops in you.

My son, attend to my words; incline thine ear unto my sayings. Let them not depart from thine eyes; keep them in the midst of thine heart. For they are life unto those that find them, and health to all their flesh.
(Proverbs 4:20–22)

❦ All You Need Is a Good Brainwashing

Set a discipline in your life. For example, I have a discipline in my life: I run. It can be raining, and I'll still put on an old hat and go out. People say, "Where are you going?" I reply, "I'm going to run." "But it's raining," they say. Well, there's nothing wrong with my legs. Why should I make the rain an excuse? It is just doing its job.

Sometimes we make other people our excuse. Husbands say, "If my wife was just a little nicer, I could be a better husband." Wives say, "If my husband would...." Husbands say, "If my wife would...." If you would both start doing, you might accomplish something and have some peace in your house and some happiness in your marriage. The best you can do is get rid of mediocrity in your own life. If you can change, then you will provoke change in other people.

Don't *expect* life to work for you, either. You need to *make* it work for you. So many people always want somebody to give them a break. I say, find a way to make a break. Break the cycle that has dominated your life. That's your break. Break laziness. Breaking these things opens a door in your life—a door of opportunity. Actually, the door to what God has promised and what He ordained for your life was opened a long time ago. When are you going to wake up and go through it?

I repeat, don't approve anything in your life that isn't excellent. Oftentimes we say that we want prosperity and to do right and do well. We're lying. We're not sincere. If we really wanted it, we would do whatever it takes to walk that way. Sincere people let nothing that opposes them prevent them. Opposition doesn't mean prevention; it means opportunity.

Many times we say, "I can't because of this"; "I can't because of that." "If I wasn't black...if I was just another color." Sometimes you have factors to deal with; but when you pursue excellence, those things can try to oppose you but can't prevent you. They opposed the first black baseball player, but he popped up anyway. Everything they opposed eventually popped up. Everything they said could not be always became. All this was in the natural! If that happens in the natural realm, then what could happen in the spiritual realm? Pray in the Spirit. Build up your faith. Get in touch with God. Let the Word of God grip your mind, and you'll get a grip on your life!

People who stay in the presence of God are always self-motivated. They always prosper no matter what job they have or what business they are in because they make joy happen. It is not the job that brings them joy; it is being in the presence of God before they ever go to the job that gives them joy. (See Psalm 16:11.) Too many people depend on this world's system and what it provides to make them happy. That's not so. Get with God like you should, and He will make you happy.

So many believers are playing games. Let me give you a piece of advice: You don't have time for games. How you allow your day to be absorbed, how you use your time, determines your productivity. Time is money, and you have to guard it. Actually, it isn't there long enough for you to say you have it. By the time you realize you had it, it's gone. That is why we are always so quick to say we don't have enough of it.

There's another characteristic of people who are excellent that we need to mention: They seek after righteousness.

☟ All You Need Is a Good Brainwashing

Proverbs 14:34 says, *"Righteousness exalteth a nation."* Both Proverbs 10:2 and Proverbs 11:4 say, *"Righteousness delivereth from death."* Proverbs 29:2 tells us, *"When the righteous are in authority, the people rejoice."* People who walk in excellence are continuously excelling in righteousness.

Let me give you two examples: Daniel and Joseph. Both Daniel and Joseph were full of excellence while still young men, teens even. Take Daniel, for instance. He wouldn't eat the king's food because it wasn't good for him. That's excellence. Later he offended some crooked governors and ended up taking their positions. That's faithfulness. (Read Daniel 6.)

If you're not faithful in your career, to those whom you serve, to the things you have to be faithful to, you won't be successful. Make it a normal endeavor to be faithful. Be excellent at being faithful—loyal, true, trustworthy, steadfast to your word, and worthy to be believed. Daniel 6:2 says that Daniel was first of the three governors over 120 princes. People who are excellent will always end up being first. They may be at the back for a while, but you can't keep them in the back forever. Think about it: Daniel was an Israelite in a Babylonian nation and government, but he was first. You can't keep people of excellence in the back. If you have goals, dreams, and desires and the spirit of excellence in your life, then it won't matter what others do. If you have a vision powerful enough, a dream strong enough, good goals, and an expectation from God, then it won't matter how many pits they put you in during your life.

You can know something that's strong enough to override and overpower the deficiencies of what you don't know, what you don't have, what isn't on your résumé, or what isn't in the bank. You might not be able to put it on paper and make it look like it will work, but you know something. I know, because I'm living proof.

People said I would never get out of Newark, New Jersey, alive. I came from a single-parent home in a neighborhood where I had to step over winos and drug addicts to go to school—and some mornings they were dead. In grade school, they said I had some type of disability. They thought something was wrong with me. I used to move around and talk a lot. I talked while the teacher was talking. Then I was a failure in high school. In fact, they told me that if I wanted to get into college, I would have to go to summer school and take three classes. If I got a C in those classes, they'd let me in. That's how terrible my GPA was and how bad my SAT scores were.

So how do you go from that to a 3.5 GPA in graduate school? It had to be God. The Spirit from God that is in you is strong enough to overcome what they say. God brought me through so I could help other people leap and hurdle and long-jump over the obstacles in life. Get enough foresight and motivation in your heart and know Who is in you. Know that because He is able to do *"exceeding abundantly above all that* [you] *ask or think"* (Ephesians 3:20), you can hurdle, long-jump, triple-jump, and leap over whatever your situation is that would otherwise hold you up in life.

In Daniel 6, all 120 princes reported to Daniel. Now, he was not even of the right race. But he was so smart, excellent, ambitious, and close to God, he had to be first. If you have the goods and you use those goods and discipline yourself, people will have to put you first. They will make you what you are supposed to be. They will make room for you. They will create a position for you. Why? It would be a disadvantage for them not to have you serving them. So they will do what they have to do in order to keep you. They'll have visions of what someone else would offer you, and they'll beat that offer.

Daniel 6:3 says that Daniel was *"preferred."* Are you preferred in your circle? If you are, anytime there is a new position opening up, you won't even have to apply; they will come and offer it to you. Now, I am not trying to brag about myself. I have been on drugs. I was an educated junkie. I was messed up, but something got in my heart. I got to the point where I decided I would walk in so much excellence that no one would beat me at what I did. For a year I was the first one to the office and the last one to leave. I took on everything no one wanted to do. After one year on that job, I went to the executive director's office and sat down. I asked him for five minutes of his time. I told him there was a position that had been open for a year and I had been doing it anyway, and I hadn't complained. I told him I felt it was time the position was given to me. I told him I felt the decision should be made within the next two weeks. Do you know what he said? "I have to advertise, but it will be just a formality."

It is how you do what you do, it is the excellence you approve, that determines the results of what you do. Excellence makes a way for you. People simply can't reject it. Now, excellence isn't something that you see on a billboard and go out and buy. Excellence is a spirit, and it comes from God. (See Proverbs 17:27; Daniel 5:12, 6:3.) Daniel was preferred because an excellent spirit was in him. The king put him over everything. What is in you? People are looking for someone they can pay to be in charge so they don't have to do it and wear themselves out.

All 120 princes and the other two presidents tried to find something wrong with Daniel, but he had drilled his life in the ways, mind, purpose, understanding, and will of God so much that they could not find fault in him. If we will grip our minds with the Word and stay in His presence, people won't be able to find fault. (See Proverbs 16:7.) A lot of times, if we would just project properly, people wouldn't see fault in us. If you walk scared and don't project excellence, people will see things in you they wouldn't have noticed normally.

Project quality at all times. Leave no signs or evidence that anything is wrong. Make it a mystery they can't solve. Drill yourself to the point that there are few or no questions asked. Project yourself in life to the point where people see the excellence and believe you speak the Word of God. Deal with your image. Sometimes the people who know you will get confused, but you need to reach more people than just the ones you know. Don't look, act, or talk like a poor person. You won't be heard. Scripture bears that out:

> *This wisdom have I seen also under the sun, and it seemed great unto me: There was a little city, and few men within it; and there came a great king against it, and besieged it, and built great bulwarks against it: now there was found in it a poor wise man, and he by his wisdom delivered the city; yet no man remembered that same poor man.* (Ecclesiastes 9:13–15)

I used to want everyone to respect me, so I tried to be extra humble. I drove a little humble car. When I went to preach driving that little car, they would throw maybe twenty dollars at me. They figured I didn't want anything. Eventually God told me that I was stupid. Now when I go preach, I pull up in either a Mercedes Benz or a limousine. I love God and I love people, but I am not playing. I have paid my dues. I am not in a rut anymore.

If you backtrack for people, if you diminish your excellence, you'll end up in a hole, and they will see that you are in a hole. That's not being like God. You can't be delivered from something or overcome something and then backslide. Don't cheat on your destiny! Don't commit spiritual adultery with that thing that had you bound. Don't go back on your standards. If you've lain in the dust, if you've slaved away in a tiny office with a sewing machine for a desk, with no heat and no air conditioning in an old dilapidated church building (like I have), don't go back.

Daniel wouldn't go back on his standards. He had a good routine: He prayed three times a day. Even when they threatened him, he still followed that routine. In the end, he prospered.

Now take a look at Joseph. In Genesis 39, Joseph was only seventeen years old, but whenever Scripture mentions him it uses the word *man*, not *boy*. Joseph acted like and produced the works of a man of God. If you want respect as a man, stop hiding in holes of bad routines that lead to ruts. Be willing to change.

Genesis 39:2 says, *"And the Lord was with Joseph."* Is the Lord with you? If He is, then Romans 8:31 says it doesn't matter who is against you. Isaiah 54:17 says no weapon formed against you will prosper.

Joseph started out as a slave in a pit. He didn't have a dime, but Genesis 39:2 also says, *"He was a prosperous man."* Remember, he was just seventeen. (See Genesis 37.)

Let's take a closer look.

> *And Joseph was brought down to Egypt; and Potiphar, an officer of Pharaoh, captain of the guard, an Egyptian, bought him of the hands of the Ishmeelites, which had brought him down thither. And the LORD was with Joseph, and he was a prosperous man; and he was in the house of his master the Egyptian. And his master saw that the LORD was with him, and that the LORD made all that he did to prosper in his hand. And Joseph found grace in his sight, and he served him: and he made him overseer over his house, and all that he had he put into his hand. And it came to pass from the time that he had made him overseer in his house, and over all that he had, that the LORD blessed the Egyptian's house for Joseph's sake; and the blessing of the LORD was upon all that he had in the house, and in the field. And he left all that he had in Joseph's hand; and he knew not ought he had, save the bread which he did eat. And Joseph was a goodly person, and well favoured.* (Genesis 39:1–6)

Whatever Joseph did, prospered. Potiphar saw that and put him in charge of everything. As a result, Potiphar prospered as well. All the time, it was the Lord and an excellent spirit that promoted Joseph.

No matter what happens, display excellence. When Potiphar's wife made a play for Joseph, he refused to compromise. (And he was at the peak of his puberty!) He ran, but because he turned her down, she lied about him to Potiphar.

&° All You Need Is a Good Brainwashing

As a result, in verse 20 the same man whom Joseph had prospered had him thrown into prison because of a lie. But the Lord was still with him. If the Lord is with you, it doesn't matter where you are—good job or bad job. What happened to Joseph? The same thing as before. The prison keeper put Joseph in charge, and everything prospered (v. 23). When you have good routines, when you display excellence, people will demote themselves and put you in charge so they can prosper.

Eventually, Joseph became second only to Pharaoh. Joseph's chariot might have been behind Pharaoh's, but Joseph was the one telling the people what to do. Pharaoh obviously thought Joseph could command Egypt better than he could. It's the same today. Successful CEOs want people around them who can do better than they can. They want to know who will make them look good.

How about you? Does the person you serve with, or work for, or work under, see that you have a good grip on your life? Can the boss put everything in your hands, leave the country, and only call in for the profits and reports? Is the place where you function blessed for your sake? Is what your hands touch prospering? If the answer is no, you need to get a grip on your life. Check for ruts and bad routines. Your leader wants to know whose hands to trust or to leave the business or ministry in, and have it prosper and multiply. Like Joseph, this is your capacity. Get a grip on your mind, and get a grip on your life. It's your destiny!

6

The Danger of Associating with Small-Minded People

6

The Danger of Associating with Small-Minded People

When I was first born again and saved by the power and Spirit of God, I associated and fellowshipped with sincere and godly people who, nonetheless, were very dedicated to their beliefs and way of thinking. Most of them were used to a small church environment of around fifty people who all believed that very few, if any, other people were saved besides them. They also discouraged reading any book—no matter who the author was—except for the Bible.

For six or seven years I suppressed the facts of my academic accomplishments for fear that if I acknowledged that I had undergraduate and graduate degrees, I would not be accepted. I never attended any developmental programs during those years because the church did not promote anything other than the services held by the church. I never heard any discussions about investing, money management, or building a degree of security and future for my family.

🎧 All You Need Is a Good Brainwashing

As I look back over twenty-five years of walking with the Lord, I wish I'd known earlier the value of being around people who know how to expand their minds and thoughts to be like His. Of course, I have no one but myself to blame for my lack of growth during those early years. Now I realize that had I expanded my associations to include people who were godly and had expanded minds, my life would have expanded too. The principle is quite simple. The people with whom we spend time are going to influence us—one way or the other.

> *Be not deceived: evil communications corrupt good manners.* (1 Corinthians 15:33)

The word *"communications"* comes from the Greek word *homilia*, which means "companionship."[1] If you associate and have extended relationships with small-minded people who limit themselves, then you will most likely be small-minded also. Don't waste your years boxed in and confined in life because you associate regularly with people who have boxed-in, confined lives. You can end up aborting your destiny if the people you spend a great deal of time with don't have God's mind or thoughts concerning you or themselves. (Again, it all goes back to getting a good brainwashing—if people don't study God's Word to find out what He says and renew their minds to the truth, they won't be able to obtain His thoughts and promises about their lives.)

In some cases, by the time you realize that you've been limited in life by limited-minded people, you've lost enough time to cause real frustration and depression. Don't give up and stay in that situation, though; find people who have God's wisdom and His thoughts to help you expand your mind from the defilement of small thinking. The bottom line is that it is to your advantage to walk and associate with people who have God's wisdom.

> *He that walketh with wise men shall be wise: but a companion of fools shall be destroyed.*   (Proverbs 13:20)

To really find your destiny and God's divine purpose for your life, you need to associate with people who have His thoughts.

The whole idea of expanding your mind by picking whom you associate with can be seen clearly in David's life. Four hundred losers who were distressed, discontented, and in debt managed to get in and associate with the right leader— David—and it changed their whole lives.

> *David therefore departed thence, and escaped to the cave Adullam: and when his brethren and all his father's house heard it, they went down thither to him. And every one that was in distress, and every one that was in debt, and every one that was discontented, gathered themselves unto him; and he became a captain over them: and there were with him about four hundred men.*   (1 Samuel 22:1–2)

> *Then they told David, saying, Behold, the Philistines fight against Keilah, and they rob the threshingfloors. Therefore David inquired of the LORD, saying, Shall I go and smite these Philistines? And the LORD said unto David, Go, and smite the Philistines, and save Keilah. And David's men said unto him, Behold, we be afraid here in Judah: how much more then if we come to Keilah against the armies of the Philistines? Then David inquired of the LORD yet again. And the LORD answered*

him and said, Arise, go down to Keilah; for I will deliver the Philistines into thine hand. So David and his men went to Keilah, and fought with the Philistines, and brought away their cattle, and smote them with a great slaughter. So David saved the inhabitants of Keilah.

(1 Samuel 23:1–5)

It's very obvious that people who associate with relentless, determined, persevering, unwavering anointed leaders become winners in spite of their previous condition of distress, debt, and discontentment. Even when they were afraid, they followed their leader and were victorious. When you look at these four hundred men, they started out with a poor résumé, but in the end, they were known as the famous and mighty men of one of the most successful kings in Israel's history! In the same way, you too can expand your life from where it is, regardless of how limited it's been, when you associate with people who have expanded minds. Sometimes you just need to make sure that the leaders you associate with and follow are expanded-minded people who can affect your mind positively.

It's simple. If you don't want your mind to be small, you must avoid small-minded people.

Keep in mind that an expanded mind leads to an expanded life. God is waiting for you to connect with His power and ability in your life. To do that, your thoughts must relate to His ability and power that works in you. *"Now unto him that is able to do exceeding abundantly above all that we ask or think, according to the power that worketh in us"* (Ephesians 3:20). The power for an expanded mind above what you've been asking and thinking is working in you right now. It's time to release it and release your unlimited future and destiny. All you need is a good brainwashing—and some people to encourage you to follow the Truth!

Do you want to win in life? Put yourself in an arena with champions. They'll be the first ones to tell you that it is going to take self-discipline. If you want to soar above the problems of life and enjoy victory, then associate with eagles. Observe the standards these people set for themselves to succeed and make yourself responsible and accountable to those same standards.

Here's some advice from an eagle—a prolific writer and preacher who consistently saw victory in his life despite his many tests.

> *We beseech you, brethren, that ye increase more and more; and that ye study to be quiet, and to do your own business, and to work with your own hands, as we commanded you; that ye may walk honestly toward them that are without, and that ye may have lack of nothing.* (1 Thessalonians 4:10–12)

Here's some more advice from another eagle—the wisest and richest man in the world, then and now: King Solomon.

> *Yet a little sleep, a little slumber, a little folding of the hands to sleep: so shall thy poverty come as one that travelleth, and thy want as an armed man.*
> (Proverbs 6:10–11)

> *He becometh poor that dealeth with a slack hand: but the hand of the diligent maketh rich. He that gathereth in summer is a wise son: but he that sleepeth in harvest is a son that causeth shame.* (Proverbs 10:4–5)

ஃ All You Need Is a Good Brainwashing

Eagles, champions, winners—they all say much the same thing. If you want to expand and succeed, you need to study, be diligent, and work at it.

There is another element in your life that is affected by the people with whom you associate—righteousness. What degree of righteousness do the people with whom you spend your time operate in? If they have little, then you will tend to decrease to their level. On the other hand, the truly righteous, according to God's standards, have divine promises of prosperity, protection, and success.

> *For the* Lord *God is a sun and shield: the* Lord *will give grace and glory: no good thing will he withhold from them that walk uprightly.* (Psalm 84:11)

> *And* [a righteous man] *shall be like a tree planted by the rivers of water, that bringeth forth his fruit in his season; his leaf also shall not wither; and whatsoever he doeth shall prosper.* (Psalm 1:3)

> *The* Lord *knoweth the days of the upright: and their inheritance shall be for ever. They shall not be ashamed in the evil time: and in the days of famine they shall be satisfied.* (Psalm 37:18–19)

> *Treasures of wickedness profit nothing: but righteousness delivereth from death.* (Proverbs 10:2)

There are many other Scriptures that declare the benefits and promises of righteousness, but even these listed here are enough for you to determine the level of righteousness around you.

The Danger of Associating with Small-Minded People ⚭

Here's something else to consider. How do those with whom you associate or surround yourself affect your self-esteem? When you're around them, do you see yourself as a ground-pecking chicken or as a high-flying, more-than-a-conqueror, victorious eagle?

Let's look again at the twelve spies that Moses sent into Canaan to spy out the land. They went in among the enemy, stayed for forty days, and then left with some fruit of the land, including bunches of grapes so large that it took two people to carry them. However, for some reason, ten of them came back with a negative confession. They infected each other and the rest of the people with a ground-pecking chicken mentality.

We came unto the land whither thou sentest us, and surely it floweth with milk and honey; and this is the fruit of it. Nevertheless the people be strong that dwell in the land, and the cities are walled, and very great: and moreover we saw the children of Anak there. The Amalekites dwell in the land of the south: and the Hittites, and the Jebusites, and the Amorites, dwell in the mountains: and the Canaanites dwell by the sea, and by the coast of Jordan....We be not able to go up against the people; for they are stronger than we. And they brought up an evil report of the land which they had searched unto the children of Israel, saying, The land, through which we have gone to search it, is a land that eateth up the inhabitants thereof; and all the people that we saw in it are men of a great stature. And there we saw the giants, the sons of Anak, which come of the giants: and we were in our own sight as grasshoppers, and so we were in their sight.

(Numbers 13:27–29, 31–33)

♋ All You Need Is a Good Brainwashing

These chickens said that the people there were too strong and the walls around the cities too large. They described in great detail the stature of the enemy that dwelled in the land. Despite the fact that God had promised it to them and even allowed them to go in for over a month and come out untouched, verse 32 says they *"brought up an evil report"* of the land they had searched. They saw themselves as grasshoppers, and, as a result, the enemy saw them as grasshoppers as well. No one is going to see you any different than how you see you!

But Joshua and Caleb had another spirit. They had infected each other with the eagle's mentality that they had received from Moses, who taught them the law of the Lord. In verse 30 Caleb said, *"Let us go up at once, and possess it; for we are well able to overcome it."* Joshua and Caleb had a strong, positive effect on each other's ability and self-esteem. They made each other winners.

Unfortunately, despite all that God had done, the people listened to the ten who spoke negatively, and the chicken mentality spread throughout the camp and caused the people to murmur and complain. It got so bad that they fearfully talked of returning to Egypt where they had been in bondage to slavery for more than four hundred years! What happened as a result of their loser confessions, lack of faith, and lack of appreciation for the miracles? They were disinherited and ended up dying in the wilderness. Can I say this again? Your associations are very important! Who speaks into your life? What kind of confession do the people around you make, especially when things get tough? Do they run or do they faint? Do they fight the good fight of faith or do they roll over and let the enemy steal, kill, and destroy them and their family? Are they pursuing the expected end God has set in place for them or do they wallow in their past?

You need to be in a visionary environment. In other words, you need to be in a place where your leader sees himself and those around him as eagles soaring to great exploits. You need to spend time where people are forcefully pushing into their divine destiny in spite of opposition. You need to be where the impossible is becoming possible; where poverty and failure are being turned into prosperity and success; where constant challenges and new endeavors are a way of life. In order to fly with the eagles, you must be in an atmosphere where more is required of you than you think you can give or perform.

Nehemiah is a great example of a visionary. Visionaries have a burden for people. In chapter 1 of the book of Nehemiah, Nehemiah was mourning, fasting, and praying because the city of Jerusalem was in ruins as a result of the disobedience of the children of Israel. He sat day and night interceding for the people of Israel, repenting for sins he himself had not committed, but that his fathers and the rest of the children of Israel had done. He reminded God of His promise that if the people would return and obey His commandments, He would gather them from where they had been scattered and set them in a place where His name dwells.

A true visionary (or leader) will stand in the gap between you and what belongs to you and seek God for your deliverance. He will remind God of His promises for obedience, teach you God's commandments, and provoke you to walk in them. Then he will teach you to understand what belongs to you as a result of your obedience so that you can walk in those promises. Actually, just having this type of leader is a promise of God as well: *"And I will set up shepherds over them which shall feed them: and they shall fear no more, nor be dismayed, neither shall they be lacking, saith the LORD"* (Jeremiah 23:4).

What happens when a true shepherd with vision begins to speak into your life with the Word of God? Your faith increases. *"Faith cometh by hearing, and hearing by the word of God"* (Romans 10:17). You learn promises like Ephesians 3:20, which says, *"Now unto him that is able to do exceeding abundantly above all that we ask or think, according to the power that worketh in us."* You learn that Daniel 11:32 says, *"The people that do know their God shall be strong, and do exploits."*

After Nehemiah had prayed and fasted, he told the king of his vision to rebuild the broken wall of Jerusalem. The king was favorable to the plan and sent men with Nehemiah to Jerusalem. In chapter 2 Nehemiah spoke about the plan that would benefit the children of Israel—they would have a wall and no longer be a reproach (v. 17). You can spot a true visionary by how his plan will benefit people outside of himself. A vision from God is not vain or selfish. It is inspired by the love of God for His people and by a burden to see deliverance in the body of Christ.

Keep in mind, though, that just because it is a vision from God does not mean that it will not require work. In fact, a true vision will require a type of work that you did not believe you could perform! It will require some exploits, especially when an adversary comes against it. I have some more news for you: Anything that will glorify God and benefit people has an adversary.

And our adversaries said, They shall not know, neither see, till we come in the midst among them, and slay them, and cause the work to cease. (Nehemiah 4:11)

The word *"work"* in this verse has a definition in the original Hebrew of "a ministry service," according *Strong's*.[2] Any "ministry service" will face some type of opposition, but remember, *"the people that do know their God shall be strong, and do exploits"* (Daniel 11:32). Philippians 4:13 says we *"can do all things through Christ which strengtheneth"* us. If that isn't enough, the Lord Jesus said, *"I give unto you power to tread on serpents and scorpions, and over all the power of the enemy: and nothing shall by any means hurt you"* (Luke 10:19). So in Nehemiah 4:15–18, we see the exploits, strength, and authority to conquer exercised with the power of God working in a "ministry service."

And it came to pass, when our enemies heard that it was known unto us, and God had brought their counsel to nought, that we returned all of us to the wall, every one unto his work. And it came to pass from that time forth, that the half of my servants wrought in the work, and the other half of them held both the spears, the shields, and the bows, and the habergeons; and the rulers were behind all the house of Judah. They which builded on the wall, and they that bare burdens, with those that laded, every one with one of his hands wrought in the work, and with the other hand held a weapon. For the builders, every one had his sword girded by his side, and so builded. And he that sounded the trumpet was by me.

Now, how else, except by the power of God, could you explain a person fighting off an enemy with one hand while building a wall with the other? Under normal circumstances, you need both hands to do either with any degree of success. How else, but by the authority given by God, could a person conquer the enemy in a battle when he is using one hand and the enemy two hands? Let's face it. They not only were using only one hand to fight, but the other hand was occupied with bricks.

Actually, they continued to build past the battle and were so focused on following the vision that they sank deep into debt. But the people had been faithful, and the shepherd spoke a word and everyone's debts were canceled. Nehemiah was appointed governor over the land, and from that point on, the local government was supernaturally provided for, without charging any taxes on the people.

A visionary will push you past your fear and lack of self-confidence. He will push past his own fear and lack of self-confidence. He will push forward when everything is against him and pursue what belongs to the people. This is what David did in 1 Samuel 30.

David was the leader of an army. They had left to fight a battle and returned home only to find their town destroyed and their wives and children taken captive by raiders. The men all cried and mourned for their families, and these men who had actually fought next to David, now talked about killing him. He was *"greatly distressed,"* it says in verse 6, but he arose and sought God. David encouraged himself, and even though two hundred of the six hundred men fainted on the way, they pursued their attackers, rescued their wives and children, and brought back the riches of their enemy. Then, like a true visionary, David shared the wealth with all of his men, even those who had stayed behind and not gone to the battle.

You may have been losing the battle all of your life, but with the power of God, you can fight the enemy even with one hand tied behind your back. You can pursue what belongs to you even in the face of heavy opposition. You may have trouble to the left, trials to the right, lack in the front, and persecution in the back, but if you will see past your immediate circumstances, you can soar like an eagle to your victory. You can fight the good fight of faith even with everything against you and never stop moving toward your destiny. And that destiny includes a victorious, prosperous, debt-free life in divine health, providing a "ministry service" to those who have need, so that others may be delivered into the glorious liberty you have as a child of God.

God has set before you the expected end of an eagle, which is to have vision keen enough to see victory past sickness, to see victory past lack, to see victory past fear, to see victory past loneliness, and even to see victory past death. Death was all around David, but he saw his victory. He knew his help came from the Lord. Where do you seek your help? Do you look to the hills, or do you look to the ground? Do you look to God as your source, or do you look to man? If you keep your face to the ground, pecking at the crumbs that life and man throw to you, then you can find the expected end the devil has for you. You'll have the same end as the chicken: You'll be eaten. An eagle's end is to eat. Will you eat the good of the land or will you die by the sword? Leave the small-minded, ground-pecking chickens alone—soar to victory with the eagles!

& All You Need Is a Good Brainwashing

Notes

[1] James Strong, *Strong's Hebrew and Greek Dictionaries* (Cedar Rapids, Iowa: Parsons Technology, Inc., Electronic Edition STEP Files © 1998), #G3657.

[2] Strong, *Hebrew and Greek Dictionaries*, #H4399.

7

Mind Expansion Causes Life Expansion

7

Mind Expansion Causes Life Expansion

lbert Einstein has been quoted as saying that he believed he used only fifteen to twenty percent of his brain capacity. And he was a genius! Since then, studies of the chemical composition of the brain cells during autopsies suggest that most people use only between six and fifteen percent of their brain capacity. So what is the rest of that eighty-five percent of the most important, most active mass in your body doing? For most of us, a large percentage of our minds is lying dormant!

There is so much potential for success and victory just waiting to be grasped. God has so many things planned for our destiny: *"Call unto me, and I will answer thee, and show thee great and mighty things, which thou knowest not"* (Jeremiah 33:3). He desires to do so many *"great and mighty things"* in us and through us. There's only one thing preventing Him: what we think.

ℰ All You Need Is a Good Brainwashing

So many people never reach their full potential in life because they restrict themselves with restricted thinking. They limit themselves with limited thinking. They stunt their growth with a grasshopper mentality.

You can't allow yourself to be limited by such a mentality. The smaller you see yourself, the smaller your life will be—and the smaller other people's perception of you will be. Stop seeing life as too big for your ability, your background, your income, your training, or anything else. The Lord Jesus Christ is able, regardless of your so-called limitations! The power to expand and stretch is already in you. (See Ephesians 3:20.) It is absolutely vital for your destiny that you push out of the grasshopper mentality and see yourself as God sees you. (All it takes is a good brainwashing!) See yourself as capable of doing all things through Jesus Christ who strengthens you! (See Philippians 4:13.)

It is truly a shame that so many sincere and well-meaning Christians remain boxed in a routine existence and in lives of limitation, failure, and defeat simply because they never challenge themselves to expand their minds to God's truth.

You will never be any more than your mind allows you to think you can be. You see, the mind is the manufacturing plant that generates the thoughts that either shrink your mind into the mold of "stinking thinking" or expand it to propel you into the abundant power, ability, and prosperity that you are capable of. Remember, that power is already in us, *"able to do exceeding abundantly above all that we ask or think, according to the power* [dunamis, 'ability...power, strength ...might (wonderful) work'[1]] *that worketh in us"* (Ephesians 3:20). Jesus' supernatural, unlimited power is available to work in us beyond what we've been asking and thinking. Unfortunately, we tend to confine the capabilities of an all-powerful, unlimited God to extremely small thinking! And all the time we are able because He is able, and we have the power because He is all-powerful.

We are made up of the things that we think the most about. *"For as he thinketh in his heart, so is he"* (Proverbs 23:7). If we want to change and take off the limits, then we need to aggressively take strong, unwavering control over the thoughts that we allow to lodge in our minds. We need to learn how to control and discipline our thoughts and make them work for us instead of against us. The Hebrew word for *"thinketh"* is *shâ'ar,* which basically means "gate-keeper."[2]

In biblical days, all the large cities and homes of people of wealth and importance had gatekeepers at the walled entrance of their estates. The gatekeeper's job was to ensure that whoever and whatever was entering and exiting the city or estate was appropriate. In the same way, we need to act as the gatekeepers of our minds. We are the only ones who can allow or prevent wrong, carnal, and negative thoughts when they attempt to enter and take up residence in our minds.

We have three primary gates that we must guard and protect: the eyes, ears, and mouth. Day in and day out our senses are bombarded with thoughts and images that can either lead us into a greater and more expansive destiny for our lives, or drain our God-given power and cause us to become ineffectual and non-productive. In short, what we allow into our minds and speak out of our mouths can bring either a blessing or a curse.

All You Need Is a Good Brainwashing

Now, don't think that you're so sophisticated that nothing can impact your spiritual relationship with God. These days nothing is as simple as it seems—not when you have an enemy who is intent on destroying you before God destroys him. Even the seemingly innocuous act of watching the evening news can send you into a depression. Why? Often we don't realize that there are demonic forces manipulating the behind-the-scenes input and impact of what we are hearing and receiving. We listen to the so-called experts, with their serious faces and cultured voices, talk about how bad things are and before we know it, we are spouting their rhetoric as the "gospel" truth.

Does this mean we should not be aware of current events? No, it doesn't. But we do need to know how to use godly wisdom in discerning what are the facts of man and what is the truth of God, for it's knowing the truth that will make us free. (See John 8:32.) For example, it's a fact that Jesus died, but the truth is He lives, and because He lives, we have been given power to be overcomers in all situations if we can expand our minds beyond how we have always thought.

Too often we put more belief in the so-called wisdom of man than the power of God. (See 1 Corinthians 2:4–5.) But it is God who has given man both the wisdom and the power to do the things he does. Remember, about eighty-five to ninety percent of our brains aren't being used. So what is it there for? It must have some God-given purpose. Maybe it's just waiting for you to be bold enough to take God at His Word and expand your way of thinking!

We can do more than what we think we can do. Success will feed and breed itself. However, so often we have to overcome the barrier of fear of the impossible. Remember the four-minute mile? Until 1954, people believed that it was physically impossible for someone to run a mile in four minutes or less, simply because it had never been documented that anyone had done it successfully. Then someone did it—and suddenly several others proved they were able to do it too. Now running a mile in less than four minutes is no longer a phenomenon.

We must learn to stop limiting ourselves to functioning by the world's standards. We do not have to be defined by what the world says we are. We do not have to limit our lives to doing what the world says we can or cannot do based on their assessment of who they think we should be. If we are the children of God, then we are no longer subject to the spirit of the world. *"Now we have received, not the spirit of the world, but the spirit which is of God; that we might know the things that are freely given to us of God"* (1 Corinthians 2:12). God has freely given us all that we need to succeed in life. But first we have to know what those things are. That is why God wants us to become spiritually mature Christians. It is also why the powers of darkness do not want us to expand our minds to their true capacity! Then we would be knowledgeable and expectant of the supernatural powers and gifts that God has declared and prepared for us and able to defeat the powers of darkness!

We need to grow up. However, until such time as we are able to desire, devour, and digest the strong meat of God's Word, we will remain spiritual babies. Now, that doesn't mean we're not saved or that God doesn't love us. Rather, spiritual babies simply are unable to receive their full spiritual inheritance because they are too weak and ignorant to handle it.

❧ All You Need Is a Good Brainwashing

Think about it. When a child is an infant, you take care of all his needs. You feed him, burp him, change his diaper, and bathe him when he's dirty because you realize that he is unable to do these things for himself. However, as that child reaches certain stages of development, you expect and encourage him to begin to do some things for himself. Even though he may make a mess when he's learning to feed himself or fall down a few times when he's beginning to walk, as a parent you encourage him to keep trying because you know it is the only way that he can learn everything he needs to know to survive.

Likewise, God encourages us as we take our first steps in seeking His truth, which helps to develop our spiritual muscles and power. *"For every one that useth milk is unskilful in the word of righteousness: for he is a babe. But strong meat belongeth to them that are of full age, even those who by reason of use have their senses exercised to discern both good and evil"* (Hebrews 5:13–14). If we don't exercise our knowledge of God's Word, our spiritual muscle and power will begin to weaken and eventually atrophy. We grow strong and become mature by continually resisting the carnality that the world tries to fool us into accepting.

The question then becomes this: Why is it that some Christians still live in the crib of infantile mentality, infantile behavior, and infantile activities, never reaching the level of productivity and destiny that God created them for? It all goes back to the mind. God sent His empowering Word to you when you first were saved, and every time you hear the Word, read the Word, and think and speak the Word of God, you are being empowered. But you will never be anything more than what you think. If you think like a baby Christian, you will remain a baby Christian. That is not God's intent. He wants to wean you away from the milk and give you strong meat to strengthen you and enable you to accomplish your true purpose. (Unfortunately, just like babies, so often we are too busy whimpering and whining to cooperate or yield ourselves to God's purpose for our lives.)

First Corinthians 2:14 goes on to say that the natural (or carnal) man is not able to receive the things of the Spirit of God. However, those who are spiritual in Christ have the very mind of Christ (v. 16), and, therefore, they are able to process and act upon the Word of God to accomplish and fulfill God's plan for their lives. So once you begin to truly nourish yourself on the meat of God's Word, you will become too big spiritually to be confined by the "crib" of your past, what the world says, or even what you have thought. Don't waste your time thinking about the world's limitations; think God's thoughts, for His thoughts for you are greater than any situation.

There is no success in your life that was not first conceived in the recesses of your mind. In the beginning, it may have been nothing more than a thought or an idea. You might not even have known why you thought it in the first place, but as you began to dwell on the idea, the possibility of it becoming a reality sparked excitement in you. Then you started to think of ways to make it happen; you began to look into the resources you would need and to network with the people who could help you make it a reality. At this point, your mind has expanded into the realm of *"things hoped for." "Now faith is the substance of things hoped for, the evidence of things not seen"* (Hebrews 11:1). You are in the realm of faith—the same faith that God used to create something out of nothing in Genesis!

✿ All You Need Is a Good Brainwashing

Too often it is at this point when limited resources, worldly restrictions, and negative input begin to distort and abort what you thought you could do. Don't allow that! Be a gatekeeper! Remind yourself, as Jeremiah did, *"Ah Lord GOD! behold, thou hast made the heaven and the earth by thy great power and stretched out arm, and there is nothing too hard for thee"* (Jeremiah 32:17). Do you know the circumstances Jeremiah was in when he came to this conclusion? He was in prison, but the word of the Lord came to him telling him to purchase land. How are you supposed to buy land when you're in jail? God had a bigger plan in mind, and although Jeremiah's situation may have seemed perilous and inconsistent with the idea of buying land, he did as God said. He expanded his mind beyond the limitations man had set upon him.

So it is with us. Sometimes the very thing that seems impossible for you to do because of your situation is the very thing you need to let God do through you to get you to your God-appointed destination. Although the situation may seem to imprison and confine you, when you expand your mind from finite and limited thinking to infinite and godly ability, you will expand your life and give spiritual birth to all the blessings that God has promised you in His Word.

Everything we are talking about here can be summed up in one way: We, as members of the body of Christ must develop a *kingdom mentality*—especially in these last days. Many Christians and so-called churchgoing religious people have very little or no idea where the kingdom of God is, or even that there is a kingdom. As a result, they go through life bound and subjugated to the demonic powers of darkness that continually plague their entire existence mentally, emotionally, physically, and spiritually. What makes it a shame is that Jesus, through His death and resurrection, has transmitted His divine, supernatural strength and deliverance from the clutches of the enemy into the lives of His kingdom heirs.

> *Strengthened with all might, according to his glorious power, unto all patience and longsuffering with joyfulness; giving thanks unto the Father, which hath made us meet to be partakers of the inheritance of the saints in light:* **who hath delivered us from the power of darkness, and hath translated us into the kingdom of his dear Son.** (Colossians 1:11–13, emphasis added)

We are heirs of the kingdom, strengthened and delivered. But do you know where the kingdom is right now?

> *The kingdom of God cometh not with observation: neither shall they say, Lo here! or, lo there! for, behold,* **the kingdom of God is within you.**
> (Luke 17:20–21, emphasis added)

The Lord's prayer in Matthew 6:9–13 has been answered; the kingdom has come! However, the next question is, do you operate in and enjoy the power and blessings of its attributes? Romans 14:17 defines kingdom traits this way:

> *For the kingdom of God is not meat and drink; but righteousness, and peace, and joy in the Holy Ghost.*

Without the righteousness, peace, and joy of the Lord, you can't maintain a kingdom mentality. You will not be able to walk in the authority that belongs to the heirs of God if you don't have these attributes operating in your daily life.

As we've mentioned in earlier chapters, righteousness has many benefits, including deliverance from death (Proverbs

10:2; 11:4). This is why the principalities and spiritual wickednesses constantly maneuver to prevent you from operating in God's righteousness. They know it destroys their ability to affect your life. A righteous man also enjoys peace (Psalm 37:37), and the joy of the Lord is our strength (Nehemiah 8:10). Keep in mind that you must search diligently to find the Word in order to have the joy of the Lord. Jeremiah 15:16 says, *"Thy words were found, and I did eat them; and thy word was unto me the joy and rejoicing of mine heart: for I am called by thy name, O LORD God of hosts."* We are called to operate on a kingdom level, but we have to find the Word to expand our minds.

In order to expand our lives as heirs of the kingdom and be victors rather than victims, we must realize and exercise the authority Jesus died for us to have. We must outgrow the religious system's lukewarm, "go to church sometimes" mentality. We must rise up in Word-centered spiritual maturity and produce the fullness and nature of Jesus Christ *"unto a perfect [teleios, 'of full age'[3]] man"* that it takes to walk in kingdom authority (Ephesians 4:13).

We must realize and remind ourselves constantly that, regardless of the opposition to our destiny as kings and priests, when Jesus died on the cross He released forgiveness for sins and gave us authority to reign in the earth.

And from Jesus Christ, who is the faithful witness, and the first begotten of the dead, and the prince of the kings of the earth. Unto him that loved us, and washed us from our sins in his own blood, and hath made us kings and priests unto God and his Father; to him be glory and dominion for ever and ever. Amen.

(Revelation 1:5–6)

And they sung a new song, saying, Thou art worthy to take the book, and to open the seals thereof: for thou wast slain, and hast redeemed us to God by thy blood out of every kindred, and tongue, and people, and nation; and hast made us unto our God kings and priests: and we shall reign on the earth.

(Revelation 5:9–10)

Jesus shed His blood so that we could walk as both kings and priests on this earth. That means we need to reign. Along with that, we need to make up our minds to be forceful about it. Jesus said the kingdom of God suffers violence (see Matthew 11:12); it's a threat to all the powers of darkness. In response we must be violent and forceful in our spiritual warfare (praise, worship, prayer, fasting, etc.) in order to keep it. We are in an eternal and permanent kingdom that faces constant opposition on this earth.

One reason we need to grow up and walk as mature kingdom heirs, maintaining our authority, in these last days is because God will demonstrate His manifested glory in the earth before Jesus returns to receive us unto Himself. (See John 14:3.) It is true that Paul said we will suffer with Him in order to reign with Him (see 2 Timothy 2:12), but he also said that our present sufferings *"are not be worthy to be compared with the glory which shall be revealed in us"* (Romans 8:18).

In order to expand your mind to walk in a kingdom mentality during these days of darkness, you must expect God to demonstrate His last-days glory in your life. You must begin to claim what the prophets foretold regarding these last days we're now in. Study Isaiah 60 carefully. Note that verse 21 says, *"Thy people also shall be all righteous: they shall inherit the land for ever, the branch of my planting, the work of my hands, that I may be glorified."*

This passage in Isaiah is truly one of the most awesome, end-time, kingdom heir, glory of God portions of Scripture available to keep our minds renewed to the reality that we are being prophetically preserved to manifest a prophetic anointing during these last days before Jesus returns. (For further awesome kingdom-glory revelation to renew your mind, read Isaiah 62 and Haggai 2:6–9.)

The key to expanding your mind is adopting a kingdom mentality. The kingdom of God is an entity, yes, but it must begin with a mentality. We must work on our minds with the Word of God. (Review Ephesians 4:23; Romans 12:2; Philippians 2:5; 1 Peter 1:13.) The way we think has everything to do with whether or not we operate in kingdom authority. We will never be more than we think. (See Proverbs 23:7.) We need to think like God. To do that, we need to know what He says about who we are because of His Son's blood. Wash your mind with this Scripture: *"Ye are a chosen generation, a royal priesthood, an holy nation, a peculiar people; that ye should show forth the praises of him who hath called you out of darkness into his marvellous light"* (1 Peter 2:9).

A vital principle for walking in dominion is living holy every day. *"Be ye holy; for I am holy"* (1 Peter 1:16).

Beloved, now are we the sons of God, and it doth not yet appear what we shall be: but we know that, when he shall appear, we shall be like him; for we shall see him as he is. And every man that hath this hope in him purifieth himself, even as he is pure. (1 John 3:2–3)

If we hope to be like Him, we should purify ourselves. That means we will set ourselves apart and make it a point to fast, pray, and seek God to eliminate impure and unholy things from our lives.

A person who doesn't sin or give in to fear, doubt, and worry or who doesn't let himself be defeated is walking in kingdom mentality. You especially need to avoid becoming a victim of things you've been delivered from previously. You must daily win the battle in your mind to remain victorious. Be a gatekeeper: Cast down negative, defeating thoughts that are against the Word of God.

If you'll keep the gate closed when the wrong thought comes along, your spirit won't be invaded. It won't be dominated by something you had dominion over! When you open your gate to fear, doubt, worry, lies, or temptation, your spirit gets contaminated. Contamination leads to corruption, and corruption leads to participation in sin. Don't participate in it. Walk in holiness. Be above sin. Know, think, and believe that you are above sin and rise to the level of authority that God gave you. Jesus is the King of Kings, and we must expand our minds to walk in a kingdom mentality to produce His very divine life.

Make no mistake—you are going to have to fight for what God says is yours. It is a matter of survival. Sometimes you have to attack first. Don't wait until you get attacked to go to battle. Remember, the kingdom of God is in us, and it suffers violence, according to Jesus. (See Luke 17:21; Matthew 11:12.) How can you survive continual violence if you never fight?

Go on the offensive. Seek God early, first thing in the morning. Don't wait until you've been beaten down by the day's events to seek Him. You are too worn out by the end of the day. Follow the principle of firstfruits when it comes to the time you spend with God. (We need to tithe from our energy and time like we tithe from our money.) In Psalm 63, David declared *"early will I seek thee....My soul followeth hard after thee"* (vv. 1, 8).

We need to delight greatly in God's commandments, like Psalm 112:1 says. To delight in His commandments means to have affection for the Word of God. If we get into the Bible and give it a chance, we will find more pleasure in it than we would ever have dreamed. Remember, Psalm 16:11 says that in God's presence is fullness of joy, and at His right hand are pleasures forevermore.

If your affections are in the right place, you will show up when God calls. When the Holy Spirit calls from inside early in the morning, you know your call to authority is coming. Get up and see what God has to say to you. A lot of people end up having bad days because they don't answer that call. Don't shut Him out. Make your body obey. Discipline yourself. The rewards include long life and peace, according to Proverbs 3:1–4, as well as ordered steps (Psalm 37:23). But you can't order your steps for the day if you don't get your instructions in the morning!

Jesus died on the cross to make sure that we have life more abundantly. (See John 10:10.) He died to give us dominion and authority to reign in the earth. He died on the cross so that we might inherit the kingdom of God. He died so that we might have all things. (See 2 Peter 1:11; Romans 8:32; 1 Corinthians 2:9–16.) With all these promises, we cannot continue to walk around defeated and limited. The kingdom of God is in us, and it is up to us to expand our minds, to maintain a kingdom mentality, and expand our lives into the destiny God ordained for us.

Notes

[1] James Strong, *Strong's Hebrew and Greek Dictionaries* (Cedar Rapids, Iowa: Parsons Technology, Inc., Electronic Edition STEP Files © 1998), #G1411.

[2] Strong, *Hebrew and Greek Dictionaries*, #H8176.

[3] Strong, *Hebrew and Greek Dictionaries*, #G5046.

8

Don't Let Double-Mindedness Destroy You

8
Don't Let Double-Mindedness Destroy You

If any of you lack wisdom, let him ask of God, that giveth to all men liberally, and upbraideth not; and it shall be given him. But let him ask in faith, nothing wavering. For he that wavereth is like a wave of the sea driven with the wind and tossed. For let not that man think that he shall receive any thing of the Lord. A double minded man is unstable in all his ways.
—James 1:5–8

What produces the "up today, down tomorrow" mentality and an insecure and intimidated feeling about tomorrow? What causes people to be in the front row of the church today shouting and dancing, and out the door not knowing where they belong tomorrow? What causes people to be in love and married today, and in the divorce court tomorrow? The answer is *double-mindedness.*

Double-mindedness is a very dangerous and destructive state of mind. James said that it causes people to be unstable in all their ways or endeavors! It would be like riding a rowboat with no oars on a choppy sea. You're down one second and up the next, with no control over the direction you'll be facing at any given moment. It's similar to what Proverbs 25:19 says: *"Confidence in an unfaithful man in time of trouble is like a broken tooth, and a foot out of joint."*

It's interesting to note that the term *"double minded"* in James 1:8 comes from the Greek word *dipsuchos,* which means "vacillating (in opinion or purpose)."[1] No wonder people change churches so often. No wonder some people can't seem to stay in a long-lasting marriage, stay in a profession, or keep a job long enough to prosper. They are victims of double-mindedness. Double-mindedness causes people to make promises they don't keep.

I have a news flash for you: Double-mindedness will lead you to failure and destruction. When your mind doesn't know which way to go, when you let it wander around, you become prone to deception. You're an easy mark for the devil. He can easily influence you with his deceptive devices of doubt, fear, and worry. It is one of the worst enemies to your success and prosperous destiny.

Double-mindedness will cause you to lose when you could win, cry when you could laugh, doubt when you could believe, hate when you could love, resent when you could forgive.

Many marriages have been destroyed because of double-mindedness. Many good businesses and ministries have been slowed down and halted because of double-mindedness. Even the corporate body of Christ has been held back from producing and experiencing the supernatural because of a large number of its ranks indulging in double-mindedness. In fact, a wavering, double mind can cause the demise of any organization—including secular ones!

How does it work? Once double-mindedness has infiltrated your subconscious or conscious thought patterns, instability is created. You become a victim of your own mind. You begin to lose control and the ability to make clear, productive decisions. The end result is failure and defeat.

But, praise God, in Christ we don't have a double mind; we have a sound mind!

For God hath not given us the spirit of fear; but of power, and of love, and of a sound mind.
(2 Timothy 1:7)

A sound mind is not split between two opinions, but secure and stable. A mind disciplined and unwavering, focused on faith-filled thoughts from the Word of God, will lead you to win in life. Why? God's thoughts and ways are stable, dependable, and victorious!

For my thoughts are not your thoughts, neither are your ways my ways, saith the LORD. For as the heavens are higher than the earth, so are my ways higher than your ways, and my thoughts than your thoughts. For as the rain cometh down, and the snow from heaven, and returneth not thither, but watereth the earth, and maketh it bring forth and bud, that it may give seed to the sower, and bread to the eater: so shall my word be that goeth forth out of my mouth: it shall not return unto me void, but it shall accomplish that which I please, and it shall prosper in the thing whereto I sent it. (Isaiah 55:8–11)

♊ All You Need Is a Good Brainwashing

It is the Word of God that you discipline your mind to think and meditate on that prospers your life. The more you train your mind to stay focused on God and His Word, the more peace and security you will experience, as Isaiah 26:3 says: *"Thou wilt keep him in perfect peace, whose mind is stayed on thee."* As you allow your thoughts to become meshed with His thoughts, your mind becomes one with His mind, and you become as sound in your thinking as God is.

However, once you receive the Word of God in your mind, you must make the determined decision not to allow negative thoughts of doubt, fear, worry, or confusion to steal or override your Word thoughts and trick you into double-mindedness. Continual study, prayer, and exposure to the anointed, spoken Word will help you guard against double-mindedness.

If, after reading this chapter, you realize that you have allowed your mind to float in and out, back and forth, and up and down in double-mindedness, it's not too late. You can change!

First, however, you must be willing to see and admit that you're unstable in your thinking. You must be willing to receive correction. Don't let double-mindedness lead you to stubbornness, which, according to 1 Samuel 15:23, *"is as iniquity and idolatry."* The spiritual principalities and rulers of darkness are doing everything they can to invade your mind and cause your belief systems to become unstable. Once you let that happen, you—and everyone around you—become subject to destruction.

After you realize what is happening in your mind and are willing to admit it, you must discipline your mind to resist the enemy's attempts to draw it away from God's truth.

Don't Let Double-Mindedness Destroy You ♋

Submit yourselves therefore to God. Resist the devil, and he will flee from you. Draw nigh to God, and he will draw nigh to you. Cleanse your hands, ye sinners; and purify your hearts, ye double minded. (James 4:7–8)

The apostle Paul gave us very specific instructions on how to identify and resist the enemy's thoughts.

Be careful for nothing; but in every thing by prayer and supplication with thanksgiving let your requests be made known unto God. And the peace of God, which passeth all understanding, shall keep your hearts and minds through Christ Jesus. Finally, brethren, whatsoever things are true, whatsoever things are honest, whatsoever things are just, whatsoever things are pure, whatsoever things are lovely, whatsoever things are of good report; if there be any virtue, and if there be any praise, think on these things. (Philippians 4:6–8)

Every time a thought comes to your mind, check it against this measuring stick. Is it true? Honest? Just? Is it pure, lovely, and of a good report? If it matches, let it in. If it doesn't, kick it out! Refuse entrance to anything that does not agree with these criteria.

When you allow fear, doubt, worry, anxiety, frustration, depression, or discouragement to camp out in your life, double-mindedness will be the result. You must override these negative emotions by wholeheartedly fighting *"the good fight of faith"* of 1 Timothy 6:12. You fight the fight of faith by meditating in and confessing the Word day and night. This step is absolutely crucial. When you fill your mind with God's thoughts, you leave no room for the enemy's. It's something you need to do every day. Without this daily step, you'll leave a crack in the door for the enemy to infiltrate. So discipline your mind and emotions to obey your commands with the Word of God. You can be in control if you want to be.

One thing these negative emotions will do is create a barrier in your mind to keep you from producing the courage and motivation you need to pursue the destiny God has for your life. Instead you'll be prone to wavering back and forth. Think what would have happened if Abraham had let his physical condition and previous track record of no heir dominate his mind. He would have never produced the miracle seed that allows us, as his heirs, to be blessed today!

Don't let life's ups and downs cause you to put more stock in your limited physical condition than in God's unlimited ability to perform what He promises. Instead, be like Abraham:

> *Who against hope believed in hope, that he might become the father of many nations, according to that which was spoken, So shall thy seed be. And being not weak in faith, he considered not his own body now dead, when he was about an hundred years old, neither yet the deadness of Sarah's womb: he staggered not at the promise of God through unbelief; but was strong in faith, giving glory to God; and being fully persuaded that, what he had promised, he was able also to perform. And therefore it was imputed to him for righteousness. Now it was not written for his sake alone, that it was imputed to him; but for us also, to whom it shall be imputed, if we believe on him that raised up Jesus our Lord from the dead.*
>
> (Romans 4:18–24)

We must be like Abraham and be fully persuaded in our thinking. We must not stagger at God's promises but force our minds into a state of full confidence and trust in His ability to deliver us and sustain us in the most difficult and seemingly impossible of circumstances. If you will do this, you will avoid the demon of double-mindedness and reach your destiny.

Sometimes your success is only a few positive, productive thoughts away. Sometimes it's just a matter of holding on and not allowing your thoughts to be altered. The longer you maintain a positive, productive thought trend, the greater your chances are for success, prosperity, and victory.

You can decide what you will think about, and stick to it no matter what else tries to divide your mind. If you will be firm, positive, and courageous, you'll destroy double-mindedness and fulfill your destiny!

Notes

1 James Strong, *Strong's Hebrew and Greek Dictionaries* (Cedar Rapids, Iowa: Parsons Technology, Inc., Electronic Edition STEP Files © 1998), #G1374.

9

Lose Your Mind to Find God's

9

Lose Your Mind to Find God's

We've talked a lot in this book about renewing our minds, thinking God's thoughts, and living the truth of God's Word despite the enemy's attacks. All of this is key to becoming successful and fulfilling our destiny.

In this chapter, however, I want to take a look at our topic from a different angle. The fact is, we need to lose our minds in order to find God's.

Most of the time, when we hear someone say they are about to lose their mind, we assume they are losing touch with sanity and reality. But we need to remember that we live in two realms—the natural and the spiritual. They're like oil and water; the two don't mix. So in order to gain the one, you have to lose the other.

When you were born again, your spirit was reborn but your mind was not. It has stayed in the natural realm. So you've got the spiritual realm in your heart, but the natural realm ruling your head. One of them is going to dominate the other.

The natural mind is limited to your human will. It's limited to what you can see, think, and feel. Frankly, it simply cannot operate in faith. Thomas, one of Jesus' twelve disciples, is known throughout Christendom for his doubting mind:

> *But Thomas, one of the twelve, called Didymus, was not with them when Jesus came. The other disciples therefore said unto him, We have seen the Lord. But he said unto them, Except I shall see in his hands the print of the nails, and put my finger into the print of the nails, and thrust my hand into his side, I will not believe. And after eight days again his disciples were within, and Thomas with them: then came Jesus, the doors being shut, and stood in the midst, and said, Peace be unto you. Then saith he to Thomas, Reach hither thy finger, and behold my hands; and reach hither thy hand, and thrust it into my side: and be not faithless, but believing. And Thomas answered and said unto him, My Lord and my God. Jesus saith unto him, Thomas, because thou hast seen me, thou hast believed: blessed are they that have not seen, and yet have believed.*
>
> (John 20:24–29)

When a natural or carnal mind is ruling, faith cannot work. It does not allow you to think beyond what you can see or experience. In fact, if you study Romans 8:5–7, you'll see that a carnal mind will lead to defeat and death. It puts you in a place where you can't operate by the power of the spiritual laws of God and succeed.

On the other hand, a spiritual mind—one that is renewed to the truth in God's Word—can tap into the power of God

Himself and experience the supernatural. It is *super*natural; it operates on a higher plane above natural facts.

If you're operating in a carnal, negative, or defeated mind, you've got to get rid of it. It will take losing the natural, human mind or way of thinking to find the supernatural, spiritual mind of God.

> *Let this mind be in you, which was also in Christ Jesus.*
> (Philippians 2:5)

When we allow the Word of God to elevate us to the spiritual realm where the mind of Jesus Christ is, we release the ability to believe and govern our lives by the same mental ability that Jesus operates with.

Paul related this unlimited ability and operation to the mind of Christ in 1 Corinthians 2:9–16. He explained how there are unlimited, unseen, unheard of supernatural things already prepared for those of us who love God. He described how the limited, natural spirit of man cannot reveal or give us the ability to know these things. But, he also showed us that there's one key element we need to find, grasp, and walk in God's thoughts and mind: the Holy Spirit. It is the Spirit who knows the mind of God. Let's take a close look at these verses.

> *But as it is written, Eye hath not seen, nor ear heard, neither have entered into the heart of man, the things which God hath prepared for them that love him. But God hath revealed them unto us by his Spirit: for the Spirit searcheth all things, yea, the deep things of God.*
> (1 Corinthians 2:9–10)

The Spirit of God already knows all that God has planned for us and is just waiting to reveal them to us. However, if we're not listening, then He can't speak. And even when we do listen, sometimes we're just "hard of hearing." Fortunately, there are some things we can do to help us become more "sensitive" to the Holy Spirit when He speaks to our spirits.

But ye, beloved, building up yourselves on your most holy faith, praying in the Holy Ghost. (Jude 20)

When we pray in the Spirit, we build up our faith. When our faith is stronger, we are more prone to hearing and believing things that we can't see or feel or touch! It will help us to listen when the spiritual mind of God attempts to reveal His thoughts, desires, and provisions to us beyond our limited natural thoughts.

We also need to exercise ourselves in the spiritual realm with prayer, study, meditation, and confession of the Word on a daily and nightly basis. If we don't, we will not be able to find and hear clearly God's mind and thoughts concerning us, even though He's speaking right from within us in our spiritual man by the Holy Spirit.

This book of the law shall not depart out of thy mouth; but thou shalt meditate therein day and night, that thou mayest observe to do according to all that is written therein: for then thou shalt make thy way prosperous, and then thou shalt have good success. (Joshua 1:8)

We must engage regularly in spiritual activities in order to be sensitive to the voice of God, speaking through the Holy Spirit, concerning things beyond our limited human mentality.

Let's continue on in 1 Corinthians 2:

For what man knoweth the things of a man, save the spirit of man which is in him? even so the things of God knoweth no man, but the Spirit of God. Now we have received, not the spirit of the world, but the spirit which is of God; that we might know the things that are freely given to us of God. Which things also we speak, not in the words which man's wisdom teacheth, but which the Holy Ghost teacheth; comparing spiritual things with spiritual. (1 Corinthians 2:11–13)

Again, it is the Holy Spirit who knows the mind of God. However, God has given us the Holy Spirit, and with Him the ability to receive, perceive, and believe what God thinks about us—or any other areas of concern beyond what our natural, human, limited mind receives, perceives, or believes. In other words, through the supernatural ability of the Holy Spirit, we can lose our minds to find God's mind, and in so doing, find supernatural opportunities for ourselves.

But the natural man receiveth not the things of the Spirit of God: for they are foolishness unto him: neither can he know them, because they are spiritually discerned. But he that is spiritual judgeth all things, yet he himself is judged of no man. For who hath known the mind of the Lord, that he may instruct him? But we have the mind of Christ. (vv. 14–16)

These verses let us know that it is critical and essential to lose our minds to find God's. In order to even receive the supernatural, unlimited things God has already prepared for us, we must get rid of our limited minds and let the mind of Christ control our existence. With the mind of Christ, which is the mind empowered and led by the Holy Spirit, God can reveal things that put our present and future life in a whole new dimension. Then we become eligible to really experience Matthew 17:20 and Mark 9:23.

> *Verily I say unto you, If ye have faith as a grain of mustard seed, ye shall say unto this mountain, Remove hence to yonder place; and it shall remove; and nothing shall be impossible unto you.* (Matthew 17:20)

> *Jesus said unto him, If thou canst believe, all things are possible to him that believeth.* (Mark 9:23)

Once you lose your mind and find God's mind, you position yourself for what used to be impossible becoming possible. You move into a realm where God can reveal Himself to you in ways and areas not even imaginable to the normal human mind. Then you are able to experience those *"exceeding abundantly above all that we ask or think"* blessings that are available when you expand your mind to the mind of God (Ephesians 3:20).

When you find His mind, His thoughts become your thoughts and His ways become your ways. When you adopt God's unlimited thoughts and ways, you become eligible for everything that God says has been freely given to you by Him.

> *Now we have received, not the spirit of the world, but the spirit which is of God; that we might know the things that are freely given to us of God.*
> (1 Corinthians 2:12).

> *He that spared not his own Son, but delivered him up for us all, how shall he not with him also freely give us all things?* (Romans 8:32)

According as his divine power hath given unto us all things that pertain unto life and godliness, through the knowledge of him that hath called us to glory and virtue. (2 Peter 1:3)

These verses make it very clear that there are things that have been given to us that we can't perceive or believe without losing our minds and finding God's mind. We won't be able to walk in these things without replacing our natural minds with the mind of Christ. Our prosperous, supernatural destiny is waiting for us if we will take on the mind of Him who promised us all things that pertain unto life and godliness.

Once you find His mind, once you have changed from the natural to the spiritual, you will find the unlimited things that have been ordained for your destiny. You will discover that He is truly able, as Ephesians 3:20 says, to do *"exceeding abundantly above all that* [you] *ask or think, according to* [His] *power that worketh in* [you]."*

10

Prosperity through a Truth-Filled Mind

10

Prosperity through a Truth-Filled Mind

No matter what went through your mind when you saw the title of this chapter, prosperity *is* part of your inheritance and destiny in Jesus Christ.

Beloved, I wish above all things that thou mayest prosper and be in health, even as thy soul prospereth.
(3 John 2)

The thief cometh not, but for to steal, and to kill, and to destroy: I am come that they might have life, and that they might have it more abundantly. (John 10:10)

Prosperity is about more than money; it's about abundant life. It includes everything from financial blessing to health in your body, from well-being in your emotions and mind to success in everything you do.

That's your heritage, but does your life match up? Are you born-again, Spirit-filled, and churchgoing but sick in your body and filled with worry about the next trouble headed your way? Are you doing all you know to do but still struggling and living from paycheck to paycheck? If so, it could be that your mind has not been filled with the truth of God's Word regarding your abundance.

Many of God's people are bound in lack, sickness, and failure because they don't know the truth of what God's Word says about them. We've always thought that such things were part of Christianity. We didn't think we were supposed to be prosperous! Who said that? Who said we weren't to enjoy the abundance that Jesus died to provide? Not the Word of God! Our lack of success is largely due to a lack of information. If we don't know what God says, then we can't walk in it. So, instead of submitting all their thoughts to the plumb line of God's promises, people simply submit all their thoughts and beliefs to whatever facts the enemy surrounds them with.

It all goes back to the mind. *All we need is a good brainwashing!* If we would learn and do what God says about our prosperity, success, and abundance, then we would not be bound to poverty, lack, and failure. We need to get free in our minds—enough to free our lives from the deception of the enemy! If we think poverty, we'll be poor. But if we follow God's methods, we'll have plenty. If we think sickness, then we'll be sick. But if we practice God's ways, then we'll walk whole. If we think failure, then we'll fail. But if we confess God's Word, we'll succeed. I ask you, what are the daily thoughts that affect your quality of life?

Jesus declared very plainly that it is the truth we *know* that makes us free.

Then said Jesus to those Jews which believed on him,
If ye continue in my word, then are ye my disciples

indeed; and ye shall know the truth, and the truth shall make you free. (John 8:31–32)

Many times finding your prosperity is just a matter of knowing you need a good brainwashing with the truth of God's Word. It is the Word of God and the truth it contains that causes your mind to prosper, which in turn prospers your life.

Beloved, I wish above all things that thou mayest prosper and be in health, even as thy soul prospereth. For I rejoiced greatly, when the brethren came and testified of the truth that is in thee, even as thou walkest in the truth. I have no greater joy than to hear that my children walk in truth. (3 John 2–4)

Notice how John rejoiced when he heard that his readers were walking in the truth. He knew that the truth would transform and empower their souls and cause or activate prosperity, or wealth and health, for their very lives. You, too, can experience your God-ordained wealth and health when you get a truth-filled mind!

When you continually feed the Word to your mind, it will empower and cleanse your mind so that you can think the way God thinks. You'll have the mind of Christ! It's our lack of thinking like God that keeps us lacking what He says we can have and be.

There's something else I want you to notice from this passage. John said that before your life can prosper, your soul must prosper.

The soul actually has five components that all have their origin and/or a connection with your mental system. When all five of those components get filled with the truth of God's Word, you are on your way to prosperity.

Your soul actually consists of your mind, your intellect, your imagination, your will, and your emotions. When each of these prosper by the truth of God's Word, your life and health will prosper, too.

For the purpose of extensive study, let's define clearly each component of your soul.

1. **Mind**. The mind refers to your basic thinking patterns. In order to prosper this component of your soul, you must consume the truth of God's Word to the point that you begin to let His mind give you His thoughts. Then you will think on *"whatsoever things are true, whatsoever things are honest, whatsoever things are just, whatsoever things are pure, whatsoever things are lovely, whatsoever things are of good report; if there be any virtue, and if there be any praise,"* as Philippians 4:8 says. You must, then, let the mind of Christ be in you as Philippians 2:5 says. As a result, prosperity and health will begin to manifest themselves in your life.

2. **Intellect**. This relates to your acquired learning and knowledge. You must learn as much truth from God's Word concerning all His promises that you can. When your intellect becomes empowered by His exceedingly great and precious promises, your soul will be empowered too, and you'll believe that you have been given all things that pertain unto life and godliness, as 2 Peter 1:3–4 clearly states.

According as his divine power hath given unto us all things that pertain unto life and godliness, through the knowledge of him that hath called us to glory and virtue: whereby are given unto us exceeding great and precious promises: that by these ye might be partakers of the divine nature, having escaped the corruption that is in the world through lust.

3. **Imagination**. Your imagination is the unlimited, unrestricted part of your mental network that allows you to leave your normal mental reference points and imagine going as far as you want to go, have as much as you want to have, and be what you want to be. It can take you right into the throne room of God without your ever leaving your physical state.

4. **Will**. The will relates to your system of desires, which will increase to the unfathomable proportions that God has in mind for you when your mind, intellect, and imagination begin to prosper by God's Word. As you process the things God says in His promises, things that belong to you, your will enlarges and you expect and desire more. Just read these:

Blessed be the Lord, who daily loadeth us with benefits, even the God of our salvation.   (Psalm 68:19)

Let them shout for joy, and be glad, that favour my righteous cause: yea, let them say continually, Let the LORD be magnified, which hath pleasure in the prosperity of his servant.   (Psalm 35:27)

And in my prosperity I said, I shall never be moved.
                                                             (Psalm 30:6)

&° All You Need Is a Good Brainwashing

Thou hast caused men to ride over our heads; we went through fire and through water: but thou broughtest us out into a wealthy place. (Psalm 66:12)

Praise ye the LORD. Blessed is the man that feareth the LORD, that delighteth greatly in his commandments. His seed shall be mighty upon earth: the generation of the upright shall be blessed. Wealth and riches shall be in his house: and his righteousness endureth for ever. (Psalm 112:1–3)

Since all these verses indicate very strongly that God desires, above all things, that you prosper and be in health, you should be motivated to prosper your soul in each of its parts. Remember, you will not prosper and be in health if your soul doesn't prosper. And that means you must continually walk in the truth you receive from the Word of God. It is the truth you know and walk in that will empower your entire soul system, including your will, and you'll begin to desire the things God's Word clearly states are yours.

5. **Emotions**. Your emotions relate to your feelings, which express what you believe. If your mind, intellect, imagination, and will are expanded to believe that you have, are, and can do exactly what God says you can do through Jesus Christ in you, then your truth-empowered feelings will declare it through various forms, including joyful and confident praise, worship, laughter, shouting, dancing, and any other form of expression!

When the emotional part of your soul is filled with the truth of God's Word, you become expressively free and can release your joy, praise, gladness, and overall celebration before you even see any physical proof of your victory or deliverance.

You'll begin to walk in total prosperity, health, and wholeness when you walk in truth in each component. Most people never receive and process enough truth in their souls to ever prosper their souls, let alone their lives. As a result, they stay bound to circumstances and experience defeat, sorrow, and failure.

Let me put a plug in here. Jesus strongly declared in John 8:32 that the truth we know will make us free. Malachi 2:6–7 states that one place we should seek truth is from the lips of God's messengers—our pastors, for example. (See Proverbs 1:14.) Maybe your prosperity hasn't come because you've missed too many truth-filled messengers. You need to do more than just stop by the church once in a while. Discipline your flesh and go to church!

The whole crux of the matter comes back to this: *All you need is a good brainwashing* with the truth of God's Word. It's not too late to find out what the Scripture says about you and your situation. If your mind has been contaminated with all the negative things—things like carnality, fear, doubt, and worry—that the thief who comes to steal, kill, and destroy brings, it just needs to be cleaned or washed out with the truth.

God has provided truth for you in His Word to prosper in you and accomplish what He has sent it to you to do. So rise up and fight a strong fight of faith with determined discipline to receive all of God's Word you can get. Make up your mind to renew your mind daily and don't compromise the schedule you set for any reason. It's not too late, so rise up as David did in 1 Samuel 30 and encourage yourself and pursue and recover all that the enemy has stolen from you with his fear, doubt, worry, and confusion. Start today to get the Word in you and let it prosper your soul and your life.

So shall my word be that goeth forth out of my mouth: it shall not return unto me void, but it shall accomplish that which I please, and it shall prosper in the thing whereto I sent it. (Isaiah 55:11)

What do you need today? Do you need healing? Psalm 107:20 says, *"He sent his word, and healed them, and delivered them from their destructions."* Do you need food? Rent money? Transportation? Philippians 4:19 says, *"But my God shall supply all your need according to his riches in glory by Christ Jesus."*

Really, it doesn't matter what we need; God has made provision for it in His Word. It's just that we've missed a lot of what God intended for us to know. We have failed to get an education, oftentimes due to money, but also because we have not had the proper contacts and exposure to the right things. For example, the body of Christ is behind financially because we haven't understood God's purpose for wealth. God intended for us to be wealthy. (Read Deuteronomy 8:18 to find out why.) We have to get past the blockage in our minds of previous thinking and look at the truth in the Word of God.

Remember, the devil is a thief according to John 10:10 and comes to steal, to kill, and to destroy us with ignorance, laziness, and disobedience. Jesus, on the other hand, says that He came that we might have life and have it more abundantly. He came with His life and replaced ignorance, laziness, and disobedience with knowledge, diligence, and obedience. Jesus came to undo what the devil did. He came and gave us the truth. He gave us His power, His anointing, and His mind. This is how we win the battle in our minds and overcome the enemy.

In Acts 1:8 Jesus said, *"Ye shall receive power, after that the Holy Ghost is come upon you."* The word *"power"* here comes from a Greek word that means "miraculous power... might (wonderful) work."[1] It is the ability of God, inherent in Christ and lent to all of His witnesses. Acts 10:38 says, *"God anointed Jesus of Nazareth with the Holy Ghost and with power: who went about doing good, and healing all that were oppressed of the devil; for God was with him."* We have that same Holy Spirit in us.

Jesus, in John 16:13, described the Holy Spirit as the Spirit of truth who would guide us into all truth. Earlier our Lord had mentioned that the Holy Spirit is our Comforter and Teacher, teaching us all things and bringing to our remembrance what Jesus had taught. (See John 14:26.) So anytime the devil brings poverty, lack, sickness, destruction, and oppression your way, let the Holy Spirit remind you of the truth in God's Word. That truth is that, no matter what comes your way, Jesus has given you abundant life.

With the power of the Holy Spirit in us, we should be sharp and wise and make good decisions. With an empowered mind filled with the truth of God's Word, we can be excellent at all we do.

In fact, the word *"abundantly"* in John 10:10 comes from a Greek word that means "superabundant...superior (in quality)...exceedingly, very highly, beyond measure."[2] As the people of God, we are supposed to be superior in quality—we're supposed to be excellent. (We've talked about this in an earlier chapter, but it bears repeating.) In Isaiah 60:15, God said we will be His *eternal excellency, a joy of many generations."* God is interested in making us His excellency, but first we have to learn the truth about ourselves in His Word. That means we should live as people of an abundant life. Our homes should be filled with the Word of God and the power of God. Whatever we do should be the best.

One of our problems is that we have become victims of excuses. I have heard people define excuses as high-class lies. I agree. Excuses have no place in a truth-filled mind. Rise up and take responsibility for yourself and change. Decide to do better. See yourself as a winner. When you see yourself as being powerful intellectually, you will even dress differently. You'll change your image and thereby make a different impression. The corporate arena understands the principle of image very well. They understand the value of what is viewed on the outside. People are reluctant to believe you are the best if you don't look the best.

Change your thinking. Start to see yourself as successful. Now, it may not seem that way to you right now, but you live by faith. (See Hebrews 10:38.) You see things that aren't yet. At the same time, the people you will need to impress may not walk by faith; they may walk by sight. They'll look at your image. So you have to understand that you need to go for and portray excellence. (See Philippians 1:10.)

Examine yourself and see what your thinking is like toward yourself and toward others. Revelation 5:9 says that God has saved us *"out of every kindred, and tongue, and people, and nation."* He doesn't see color. Do you? Learn to treat people well, no matter what. A lot of people have been mistreated in their lives, and wherever they find freedom, love, liberty, and cordiality, they will remember. Who knows how your excellence with them will affect the world?

Remember the Samaritan woman in John 4? She had several nationalities in her background besides being Jewish. And at the time Jesus and His disciples met her, she'd been married five times and was living with another man. Jesus wanted to deliver her; the disciples had a problem with her. But Jesus took the time to minister to her. That touched her so deeply that she returned to her city and got everyone to come back with her, wanting to know Jesus. His ministry to one person resulted in the evangelizing of a whole city!

No one is too low. Jesus Christ is the head of one body. The world has lied to us, teaching us things like segregation. Romans 12:3 says to let no man *"think of himself more highly than he ought to think."* Don't miss your prosperity because of your hang-ups.

Again, don't see yourself as lower than you ought. You are never inferior to anyone unless you think you are. Now, sometimes people may treat you as an inferior, but that's because they're afraid of you. That's what happened to Joseph. His brothers sold him into slavery in Egypt to get rid of him, but instead of saying, "I'm a slave; I'm no good," he rose up and worked hard. He pursued excellence, and the Lord was with him and prospered him even in the midst of those circumstances.

You may ask at this point, "What about trials? If we're to have an abundant life, why do we run into tests and trials?"

All You Need Is a Good Brainwashing

When you go through trials in your marriage, career, business, or health, the enemy would have you believe that God has left you to fend for yourself. That's not so. Hebrews 13:5 says that He will never leave us or forsake us. Instead, the truth about our trials is found in Isaiah 48:9–10:

> *For my name's sake will I defer mine anger, and for my praise will I refrain for thee, that I cut thee not off. Behold, I have refined thee, but not with silver; I have chosen thee in the furnace of affliction.*

God has not cut us off. Rather, He refines us, not with easy things such as silver, but He has chosen us in the furnace of affliction. Let's look at some of these words a little more closely so that we can clearly see the truth of what God is doing.

The word *refined* comes from a Hebrew word that indicates a purification process that uses heat, similar to the process gold goes through when it is melted for purification.[3] At the same time, the word *chosen* comes from a Hebrew word that means "acceptable…excellent."[4]

Do you see what God is doing here? God is looking for excellence. Our job is to stay focused on our assignment through the trial. We need to remember the truth: God's thoughts toward us are thoughts of peace and an expected end. (See Jeremiah 29:11.)

If we want excellence in our lives, again, it all goes back to getting the truth in our minds. We must make study of the Word of God, prayer, fellowship with God, and family devotions a regular part of our household. Let's spend some quality time getting the truth.

Prosperity through a Truth-Filled Mind

When you follow the truth, prosperity will come. It did for Joseph, and it did for Daniel as well.

Daniel was preferred above the presidents and princes, because an excellent spirit was in him; and the king thought to set him over the whole realm. Then the presidents and princes sought to find occasion against Daniel concerning the kingdom; but they could find none occasion nor fault; forasmuch as he was faithful, neither was there any error or fault found in him.

(Daniel 6:3–4)

Notice two things: Daniel had an excellent spirit, and he was faithful. People of truth are excellent and faithful. They don't whine and complain. When you whine and complain, you start to make excuses. Remember how we defined excuses? You are only one step away from lying. Philippians 2:14–15 says, *"Do all things without murmurings and disputings: that ye may be blameless and harmless, the sons of God, without rebuke, in the midst of a crooked and perverse nation, among whom ye shine as lights in the world."* Sons and daughters of God, filled with truth, do everything with a positive attitude. Your life should show forth a light and hold up the truth of the Word of God. Let me get practical here for a second. You can't say that you are full of God and full of the truth when you cannot cooperate with your coworkers. The life of Jesus should be manifest in your mortal flesh, but the life of Jesus is not manifested in coming in late for work. That's not excellence!

Remember, God intended for you to be the best. Sin and failure were never supposed to be a part of our lives, but when Adam sinned, he brought those things into existence. Glory to God, though, Jesus came to eradicate that! *"For he hath made him to be sin for us, who knew no sin; that we might be made the righteousness of God in him"* (2 Corinthians 5:21). That was a great gift. Unlimited riches and prosperity come through that one gift.

The church has tried, but people haven't heard a lot about prosperity. So far we have not gotten much further than "spiritual" needs. Ministers haven't been teaching a lot about practical prosperity. The truth is, your life with Jesus goes much further and much deeper than repentance at the altar. As a people, as the body of Christ, we have to know about money. We need excellence in regards to our finances.

The Scripture says that *"his divine power hath given unto us all things that pertain unto life and godliness, through the knowledge of him"* (2 Peter 1:3). Let me remind you that it takes diligence. If you're lazy, you won't experience those things. If you are not honest and upright, you won't receive. Psalm 84:11 says that the Lord God is a sun and a shield; He gives grace and He gives glory, and He withholds no good thing from those who walk upright.

All this means we don't have to live on "Failure Boulevard," "Barely Get Along Lane," or "Hobo Drive." Such great and precious promises as He has given don't yield a mediocre or even an average existence. They yield excellence. But we have to be partakers of His divine nature. We have to partake of the divine power that gives us all things. We have to add diligence to our faith all the time, not just when we feel like it—everywhere and in every situation.

The truth has to be uncovered. Second Corinthians 4:3 says that if the Gospel (truth) is hidden, it is hidden to those who are lost. People are lost in failure, sickness, poverty, anxiety, and low self-esteem because that which heals, delivers, and prospers is hidden. People are saved, but certain critical truths are hidden. Let's face it, if you haven't found it, then it is hidden.

People who are lost cannot find their destiny. People who are lost cannot find their prosperity. If you do not know the truth, then anything that truth provides for you is lost to you until you know the truth. A lot of Christians have lost prosperity. The truth says, *"For ye know the grace of our Lord Jesus Christ, that, though he was rich, yet for your sakes he became poor, that ye through his poverty might be rich"* (2 Corinthians 8:9). Psalm 112:3 says, *"Wealth and riches shall be in his house* [the house of a man who fears the Lord]: *and his righteousness endureth for ever."* Deuteronomy 8:18 declares, *"It is* [God] *that giveth thee power to get wealth, that he may establish his covenant which he sware unto thy fathers, as it is this day."* A lot of Christians do not know these things. That is why they are not free. If you didn't know them before, now you do. Make sure you fix your heart on them. Make sure you know the truth—the truth about your heritage and destiny of total prosperity—spirit, soul, and body.

> *And the very God of peace sanctify you wholly; and I pray God your whole spirit and soul and body be preserved blameless unto the coming of our Lord Jesus Christ.* (1 Thessalonians 5:23)

◕ All You Need Is a Good Brainwashing

Notes

[1] James Strong, *Strong's Hebrew and Greek Dictionaries* (Cedar Rapids, Iowa: Parsons Technology, Inc., Electronic Edition STEP Files © 1998), #G1411.

[2] Strong, *Hebrew and Greek Dictionaries*, #G4053.

[3] Strong, *Hebrew and Greek Dictionaries*, #H6884.

[4] Strong, *Hebrew and Greek Dictionaries*, #H977.

11

It's Time to Release Your Mind to Your "Wealthy Place"

11

It's Time to Release Your Mind to Your "Wealthy Place"

Thou hast caused men to ride over our heads;
we went through fire and through water: but thou
*broughtest us out into a **wealthy place**.*
—Psalm 66:12, emphasis added

It's time to start releasing your mind to your unlimited wealthy place. When your mind is totally convinced that in God you have no limitations in any area of life, then your lifestyle will expand. Your living conditions will improve. Your career will take off. Your income and finances will increase. This is God's will for you; it is His plan that you fulfill His prophetic will and destiny for your life!

Your life and circumstances will never change, though, until you set your mind for increase. You must renew your mind and believe there is an unlimited, wealthy place of increase for you based on your righteousness in Jesus. You must stand up and proclaim for all to hear—including the devil—that this is the hour for God to increase you more and more!

It doesn't matter how long you've been in your limited situation and lack. Release your mind! Start shifting your mind into high gear and start releasing it into your wealthy place. It is God's promise to you and to your children.

> *The LORD hath been mindful of us: he will bless us; he will bless the house of Israel; he will bless the house of Aaron. He will bless them that fear the LORD, both small and great. **The LORD shall increase you more and more, you and your children.** Ye are blessed of the LORD which made heaven and earth.*
>   (Psalm 115:12–15, emphasis added)

And let's repeat our opening verse:

> *Thou hast caused men to ride over our heads; we went through fire and through water: but thou broughtest us out into a **wealthy place**.*
>   (Psalm 66:12, emphasis added)

Your wealthy place is where you've freely been given all things that pertain unto life and godliness through Jesus. (See 2 Peter 1:3; Romans 8:32.) Your wealthy place is where all God's promises are "yea and amen." (See 2 Corinthians 1:20.)

Do you realize how much God desires to enlarge the place of your tent, or in other words, your life? He wants to break your life out on the left and on the right. This is your time for enlargement and increase! No matter how much failure, hurt, and shame you've gone through, now is your time to come out of it all! Start releasing your mind to think on things that are good, lovely, honest, virtuous, pure, and of good report, as Philippians 4:8 clearly instructs, and you'll find yourself experiencing things from the Word of God that are good, lovely, virtuous, pure, and of good report.

If you have to, stretch your mind out of depression, worry, doubt, fear, self-pity, loneliness, hurt, embarrassment, or any other negative emotion that has locked down your mind, and start claiming the truth of God's prophetic word for your life.

Enlarge the place of thy tent, and let them stretch forth the curtains of thine habitations: spare not, lengthen thy cords, and strengthen thy stakes; for thou shalt break forth on the right hand and on the left; and thy seed shall inherit the Gentiles, and make the desolate cities to be inhabited. Fear not; for thou shalt not be ashamed: neither be thou confounded; for thou shalt not be put to shame: for thou shalt forget the shame of thy youth, and shalt not remember the reproach of thy widowhood any more. (Isaiah 54:2–4)

It's time! It's time for your life to enlarge and break out on all sides and for your expansion to come! God has promised you great increase if you'll start releasing your mind. No matter how small and unproductive your life has been in your business, career, ministry, or any other endeavor, God wants to give you great increase. Don't get weary in well-doing, for you will reap in due season if you don't faint. (See Galatians 6:9.) This is your time and your season; your changes, prosperity, and increase are just a "brainwashing" away. *All you need is a good brainwashing.*

Job had something to say about the great increase that is coming your way, that even now is knocking on the door of your heart:

♋ All You Need Is a Good Brainwashing

*If thou wouldest seek unto God betimes, and make
thy supplication to the Almighty; if thou wert pure and
upright; surely now he would awake for thee, and
make the habitation of thy righteousness prosperous.
Though thy beginning was small, yet thy latter end
should greatly increase.* (Job 8:5–7)

When your heart is pure, when you seek God with all
your heart, soul, and mind, when you fill your mind with His
eternal, prophetic Word, you will be an open vessel in which
all the promises of God can be fulfilled.

Once you release your mind to your wealthy place and
begin to think the wealthy, prosperous way that God's Word
declares He has ordained for you, you'll begin to see that
whatever you do will prosper. You must renew your mind to
the fact that God has pleasure in your prosperity and that He
will send prosperity to you now!

*Blessed is the man that walketh not in the counsel of
the ungodly, nor standeth in the way of sinners, nor
sitteth in the seat of the scornful. But his delight is in
the law of the Lord; and in his law doth he meditate
day and night. And he shall be like a tree planted by the
rivers of water, that bringeth forth his fruit in his season;
his leaf also shall not wither; and **whatsoever he doeth
shall prosper.*** (Psalm 1:1–3, emphasis added)

*Let them shout for joy, and be glad, that favour my righ-
teous cause: yea, let them say continually, Let the Lord
be magnified, which hath pleasure in the prosperity of
his servant.* (Psalm 35:27)

*Save now, I beseech thee, O Lord: O Lord, I beseech
thee, send now prosperity.* (Psalm 118:25)

Spend quality time meditating on the Word of God so you can release your mind. Everything the Word of God says is yours is yours, especially if you discipline your mind to think in a wealthy and prosperous way as God does. God wants you to get to your wealthy place so you can be a blessing to the kingdom of God and humanity.

It's time for you to release your mind to your wealthy place! There's only one thing that will try to stop you—and that's the devil.

With that in mind, let's go over some of what we've learned in this book.

The devil knows there is greatness in you. He knows who has the Holy Spirit. He knows who has the dynamite. And he's going to do everything he can to invade your mind with fear, anxiety, sickness, and anything else he can use. His only purpose is to steal, kill, and destroy. He is out to destroy you and anyone who has anything to do with you.

First Peter 5:8 says that our adversary is like *"a roaring lion, walk*[ing] *about, seeking whom he may devour."* He really wants to drive us crazy so we shift our focus off of God and His Word. There are so many things in life he can use to drive us crazy. He knows he only has to aggravate us a little bit in our physical health, in our marriage, or in our finances, and our minds will experience worry, anxiety, and stress. So, he sets out to get our minds off of God however he can.

The devil is going to try to use people against you. Who are you associating with? You can't fly with eagles while pecking with the chickens. You'll never soar in life as long as you spend time down in the barnyard. Our ultimate position in life is to soar above the storms and occupy a position of dominion and authority. Chickens don't do that. They never get up off the ground—unless it's to end up on the table as someone's meal.

Maintain relationships with people who are releasing their minds to their wealthy places. Find those who desire to soar, who are already soaring, and who have unlimited expectations for their lives. Get together with some big dreamers—they're going to their unlimited wealthy place!

> *But they that wait upon the LORD shall renew their strength; they shall mount up with wings as eagles; they shall run, and not be weary; and they shall walk, and not faint.* (Isaiah 40:31)

> *Who forgiveth all thine iniquities; who healeth all thy diseases; who redeemeth thy life from destruction; who crowneth thee with lovingkindness and tender mercies; who satisfieth thy mouth with good things; so that thy youth is renewed like the eagle's.* (Psalm 103:3–5)

You can soar as the eagle to your unlimited wealthy place if you will renew your mind daily with all the promises and truth found in the Word of God.

The devil will try to keep us down with low self-esteem and a low sense of self-worth. So often we fall into his trap and fail to associate our lives with the greatness God has ordained for us. God has a power inside us that is greater than our problem! If your problem seems to be heavy, I have news for you: It's really light. *"For our light affliction, which is but for a moment, worketh for us a far more exceeding and eternal weight of glory"* (2 Corinthians 4:17).

We might not count that problem light, but God does. And He's the one carrying it anyway. If we really were carrying it, we'd be wiped out the first day. God, on the other hand, is carrying it, and He's still able to move.

Because God is the one carrying your *"light affliction,"* you are still in the race. God is not through with you yet. *"Being confident of this very thing, that he which hath begun a good work in you will perform it until the day of Jesus Christ"* (Philippians 1:6). It may not look like it, but God is still working with you. He's made you a new creature, and it's His greatness in you that does it.

Another thing the devil uses against us is our lack of knowledge. We go through a lot of things because we lack knowledge. Hosea 4:6 begins by saying, *"My people are destroyed for lack of knowledge."* Then it goes on to say it is because we rejected knowledge. Because we have rejected the knowledge available to us through preaching, teaching, prophecy, and the voice of the Holy Spirit to us in our personal study, we will be rejected. According to 1 Peter 2:9, we are a *"royal priesthood,"* but Hosea 4:6 also says that we will no longer be priests to God when we reject knowledge. What we don't know can cause us to be destroyed.

The enemy also attempts to discourage you through trials. But Isaiah 59:19 says, *"When the enemy shall come in like a flood, the Spirit of the LORD shall lift up a standard against him."* When you are under attack from the enemy, your standard is faith, your standard is patience, your standard is longsuffering. In short, your standard is Colossians 1:11: *"Strengthened with all might, according to his glorious power, unto all patience and longsuffering with joyfulness."*

All You Need Is a Good Brainwashing

God is trying to show the devil that His standard is in you! God will prove, through your trial, that He is God. There is greatness in you, and God is trying to get it out. It may take a series of exercises to find it, but God will prove that the greater one is in you. Whatever you are dealing with, rest assured that God is working in your situation. It is difficult to go through a trial, but if you know what God says, even when the fire is seven-times hot, you won't be burned.

> *When thou passest through the waters, I will be with thee; and through the rivers, they shall not overflow thee: when thou walkest through the fire, thou shalt not be burned; neither shall the flame kindle upon thee.*
> (Isaiah 43:2)

God hasn't left you. He was there before, and He is still there now. Hebrews 13:5 says, *"I will never leave thee, nor forsake thee."* And because He is right there, your miracle is right there. It's not settled. It's not over. Nothing is decided yet. God is the only One who can settle anything. The doctors (thank God for them) can't settle anything. God is the only One who has the final say.

The devil is going to try to throw every negative thing he can at your mind. When he can affect your mind to the point where your mood is altered, you become vulnerable to his tricks. Before you know it, what he does will seem more real than reality. He knows that if he can affect your thinking, he can affect your life.

Actually, it doesn't matter to him how he gets you as long as he gets you. You see, the devil can't bother God, so he'll bother those who have His greatness in them. If he can bother you, if he can get you off of God's Word, then he can say to God, "See? I got them to doubt You." That's what he tried to do with Job. He wants to be able to go to God and say, "See? I got them to talk negatively. I got them to talk against You. I can affect them more than You can."

He wants to affect you enough that you destroy yourself. He wants to turn you against God and against yourself so that you never release your mind into your wealthy place. He wants to thwart the relationship you have with God by stealing what you have with Him in your mind.

Praise God, though, He has given us everything we need to win the battle and fulfill our destiny! For one thing, He has given us His Word. If we hear the Word enough, it will cause us to rise to a level of faith above every plot of the enemy. Romans 10:17 says that faith comes *"by hearing, and hearing by the word of God."* If we hear the Word of God enough, the anointing of God will destroy any yoke in our lives. (See Isaiah 10:27.) The anointing works beyond our feelings, beyond our situations, beyond what we want or don't want.

Matthew 4:4 and Luke 4:4 both say that we are to live by every word that comes out of the mouth of God. Hebrews 2:1 admonishes us to *"give the more earnest heed to the things which we have heard, lest at any time we should let them slip."* Don't let the Word slip; you have to live by God's every word. This is key in getting to your wealthy place. What have you let slip already? You can't live by every word if you don't know every word.

You have to know what God says. Even when you don't know what to do or what to say, you have to know what God says. God has already said what He has to say. The only ones talking now are you and the devil. The devil is telling you it's over. What are you saying to him? If you want to shut the devil up and cut him off, then tell him what is written. That's what Jesus did. Jesus was approached three times by the devil, and He told him only what was written. (See Matthew 4 and Luke 4.) The devil tried to tempt Jesus three times, and every time He responded with what God had said.

No matter what we go through, we have a mandate on our lives to know what God has said. No matter how many times the devil comes to our minds and says we're going to die, we have to be able to say, "Oh no, devil, Psalm 118:17 says *'I shall not die, but live, and declare the works of the LORD.'* Don't talk to me anymore about dying. I'm too busy living and declaring the works of the Lord. God has a wealthy place for me, and you are not going to trick me out of my destiny."

You have to resist based on what you know. Since you know you have the greater one in you, even though the lesser one is talking, position yourself in your wealthy place with what you know.

Actually, the enemy attacks you because of what you know. His plan is to try and get you to say something other than what the Word of God says. If he can get you to say "I think I'm delivered" or "I hope I'm delivered" instead of "I know I'm delivered," then you will end up in deep unbelief. Unbelief causes you to be destroyed because then you don't know anymore. You will be attacked for what you know, but what you don't know might kill you.

Even if we do forget the Word, God has given us another Helper, the Holy Spirit, who will bring it to our remembrance. (See John 14:26.) We have to tap into the Holy Spirit. Jude 20 says we should build ourselves up on our most holy faith, praying in the Holy Spirit. That way we can discern when we are under attack!

First Peter 5:8 warns us to *"be sober, be vigilant."* That means to be watchful, stable, sound, and steadfast in our minds. We can't let anything but the Word into our heads. When we are filled with the Word of God, we'll know when we are under attack. When we're prayed up, we'll recognize the enemy's devices. We have to pray and fast ahead of time. Our minds need to be prepared. If we will fill our minds with the truth of God's Word, there won't be room for anything else. The question is, do you want to walk above what is trying to overtake you? Do you want to overcome it or do you want to remain under it? You are in control of what goes on inside you. I've never seen a joint yet that jumps in your bed, wakes you up, and forces its way into your body.

When the devil says, "You're defeated," be ready to say, "I have already overcome *'because greater is he that is in* [me], *than he that is in the world'* (1 John 4:4)." When the liar says you can't, be ready to say, "It's not my ability, but the ability of Jesus; *'I can do all things through Christ'* (Philippians 4:13)." You have to be prepared to resist the devil. James 4:7 says, *"Submit yourselves therefore to God. Resist the devil, and he will flee from you."* He will run in terror, but we have to submit ourselves to God to stand against the devil. It is better to get the Word in us before the attack. Preventative maintenance is always better.

Trying to get a vaccine after you already have the disease won't work. Have a daily prayer life. Be the gatekeeper over your thoughts. Don't let negative things into your mind. You are the captain of your ship. Don't let the devil get the peace out of your mind. Isaiah 26:3 says God will keep him in perfect peace, whose mind is stayed on Him. If your mind is stayed on Jesus, you'll stand firm like Jesus—stand in your conviction, stand in your position with God—and hold fast to the confession of your faith without wavering because you know that He who promised is faithful. (See Hebrews 10:23.)

Beyond what the devil says, you have to know what God has to say. And He says there is greatness in you. You need to realize this. Now, you have this greatness not because of you, but because of Jesus in you. He is the First and the Last, the Beginning and the End, the Alpha and Omega, the Author and the Finisher of our faith. He is the One who took our infirmities and bore our sicknesses. He was the One wounded for our transgressions and bruised for our iniquities. The chastisement of our peace was upon Him, and it was by His stripes we were healed. (See Isaiah 53:4–5.) That is without question. He is the One who did it all. He is the One who gave us righteousness, divine health, and the power to get wealth. These things are all in your wealthy place!

God also has given us pastors, shepherds, priests. Make sure you have a pastor in your life who is not afraid to preach the Word that frees people from the bondages in their lives. If you were in the gutter last night, your pastor can't be afraid to say, "Stay out of the gutter!" He can't worry about what you think because there may be hundreds of others who would end up in the gutter if he didn't speak the truth. Pastors need to preach the truth of the Word of God so people can learn to avoid the traps and pitfalls the enemy puts into their lives.

Fasting also can stop the enemy in his tracks. Do you want to keep him from getting into the minds of your children and influencing them? Turn down your plate and pray. If you will fast and pray, then the God who cannot lie, according to Titus 1:2, will perform what He has declared in Isaiah 58:6–12:

> *Is not this the fast that I have chosen? to loose the bands of wickedness, to undo the heavy burdens, and to let the oppressed go free, and that ye break every yoke? Is it not to deal thy bread to the hungry, and that thou bring the poor that are cast out to thy house? when thou seest the naked, that thou cover him; and that thou hide not thyself from thine own flesh? Then shall thy light break forth as the morning, and thine health shall spring forth speedily: and thy righteousness shall go before thee; the glory of the LORD shall be thy rereward. Then shalt thou call, and the LORD shall answer; thou shalt cry, and he shall say, Here I am. If thou take away from the midst of thee the yoke, the putting forth of the finger, and speaking vanity; and if thou draw out thy soul to the hungry, and satisfy the afflicted soul; then shall thy light rise in obscurity, and thy darkness be as the noon day: and the LORD shall guide thee continually, and satisfy thy soul in drought, and make fat thy bones: and thou shalt be like a watered garden, and like a spring of water, whose waters fail not. And they that shall be of thee shall build the old waste places: thou shalt raise up the foundations of many generations; and thou shalt be called, The repairer of the breach, The restorer of paths to dwell in.*

If you will fast for the right reasons, stop criticizing people, stop pointing fingers, and get your life right with God, the oppressed will go free, bread will be dealt to the hungry, the afflicted soul will be satisfied, and your health will spring forth speedily. Every yoke, every bondage, everything the devil tries to do to people, will be broken.

God has a destiny for everyone in the body of Christ, and we have to get there together. We in the church have to be reinforcements for each other. We can't stand back and watch each other go through hell. God will not release your wealth if you are selfish. Just because it is not you today, doesn't mean it won't be you tomorrow. *"We then that are strong ought to bear the infirmities of the weak"* (Romans 15:1). If you don't step in to help someone when it is his time, then when your turn comes to go through, you will wish you had prayed for somebody.

If we will bind ourselves together, if we will carry one another's burdens and really get concerned for one another in the body of Christ, if we will get our lives centered on the Word of God, the devil won't be able to take any of us out. If he attacks one of us, he attacks all of us. If one laughs, we all laugh. If one mourns, we all mourn. The church has to rise up or we'll keep having holes in the boat and the whole vision will sink.

Prayer is so important. You have to learn that, when the mood hits you to fall into temptation, you can pray not to enter into temptation. In Matthew 26:36–45, Jesus went through the same thing. He said His soul was *"exceeding sorrowful"* (v. 38). He said, *"Father, if it be possible, let this cup pass from me"* (v. 39). His flesh didn't want to go to the cross. Nevertheless, He went through. The flesh was weak, but the spirit willing, so He said, "Let Your will be done."

Pray that you enter not into temptation. Pray that you enter not into doubt. Pray that you enter not into fear when your body is going through pain and suffering. Jesus suffered all of that at one time. I can see Him in my mind's eye. I can see Him going through, His flesh going through, His soul vexed, and He's praying. Pray that you enter not into temptation. Pray that you don't give in.

Whatever you are going through right now, whatever is "whipping" on you right now, don't let go. Don't quit. Jacob didn't. He wrestled all night and said, "I won't let you go until you bless me." (See Genesis 32:26.) Until your situation is rectified, don't let go. Don't ever let go of God. God will help you. But you have to cast down all imaginations that exalt themselves above the knowledge of God as 2 Corinthians 10:3–5 says. *"For the weapons of our warfare are not carnal, but mighty through God to the pulling down of strong holds"* (v. 4). Our weapons are not of the flesh, and it's the flesh—the mind—that is under attack right now.

You see, you had the nerve to get saved and delivered. You had the nerve to praise God. And before you can influence someone else, the devil wants to get you back where you were. He doesn't want that greatness in you to manifest. He is afraid you will influence others to follow you out of the crack house, out of poverty, out of lack, out of fear and doubt. He doesn't want you to win because you would influence someone else to win and reach the destiny God has for him or her.

> *But ye are a chosen generation, a royal priesthood, an holy nation, a peculiar people; that ye should show forth the praises of him who hath called you out of darkness into his marvellous light.* (1 Peter 2:9)

The enemy doesn't want you to show forth the praises of God to the people around you, so he attacks you. But, when you show forth the praises of God even when you're under attack, you seal your victory. When you continue to praise God in the midst of defeat, you drive the enemy backward.

Above all, it takes *discipline.* Hebrews 2:1 says that *"we ought to give the more earnest heed to the things which we have heard."* That means we should give intense attention to what we are taught lest at anytime we let it slip. God will require that you show what you have heard by what you do. You need to act on the Word.

It's time to release your mind to your unlimited, wealthy place. First John 4:4 says, *"Greater is he that is in you, than he that is in the world."* Your broken heart may seem great, but greater is He that is in you. Your problem may feel overwhelming, but greater is He that is in you. Your situation may feel out of control, but greater is He that is in you. Your health problem may feel unconquerable, but greater is He that is in you. Your financial problem may loom large, but greater is He that is in you. Your bills may be piled high, but greater is He that is in you. Your loneliness may threaten to swallow you, but greater is He that is in you. Your stress may seem like it's about to drown you, but greater is He that is in you. Your confusion may feel intense, but greater is He that is in you. No matter what is in your life right now, no matter what he who is in the world has put in your path to trip you, greater is He who is in you than he who is in the world. Win the war in your mind. Tear down the walls of limitations. Avoid carnality. Remove the stumbling blocks. Soar with the eagles. Get rid of double-mindedness. Now is the time to release your mind to your wealthy place. Fulfill your destiny!

All you need is a good brainwashing.

About the Author

Dr. Frank and Pastor JoeNell Summerfield are the founders of Summerfield Ministries, Word of God Fellowship Church, and Word of God Christian Academy, located on a 120-acre site in the Raleigh, North Carolina, area. In addition to managing over eighty full-time paid staff, they continue to travel extensively throughout the world, boldly ministering the uncompromised Word of God.

The sincere desire at Summerfield Ministries is to develop a high quality of life in people of all racial, ethnic, and socio-economic origins. Pastors Frank and JoeNell Summerfield minister to the total man and woman—spirit, soul, and body. Together with God's divine direction and the Holy Spirit, they spread the positive, life-changing message of the Gospel locally, regionally, nationally, and internationally. Summerfield Ministries can be seen on Court TV as well as many Christian cable stations throughout the country.

All You Need Is a Good Brainwashing is the latest in the extensive list of books Dr. Summerfield has authored. Some of his other titles are *Knowing Our Delegated Authority, God's Formula for Personal Success and Prosperity, How to Make Your Marriage Produce Fruit, How to Avoid Life's Sex Traps,* and *Leaders Who Serve Leaders.*

The Summerfields have four children, all of whom are involved and supportive of the ministry.

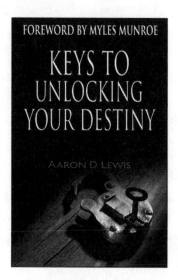

ANOTHER POWERFUL BOOK

from Whitaker House

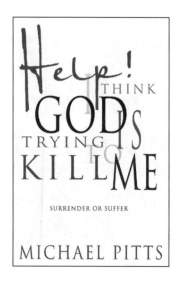

Help! I Think God Is Trying to Kill Me

Michael S. Pitts

Are you dying to become the man or woman God wants you to be?
Then join Pastor Michael Pitts where the rubber meets the road as
he tackles issues of identity, fear, bitterness, brokenness, and negative
confessions. This book is for anyone anxious to live beyond mediocrity
and experience the miraculous. It is milk for those who need to go
gently into a spirit-filled life, and a hearty meal for the every mature
believer searching for a deeper level of communion and commitment.

ISBN: 0-88368-774-7 • Trade • 240 pages

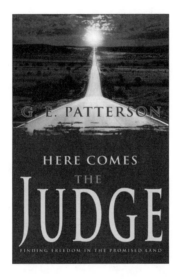

OTHER POWERFUL Books

from Whitaker House

Understanding the Purpose and Power of Woman
Dr. Myles Munroe

To live successfully in the world, women need to know who they are and what role they play today. They need a new awareness of who they are, and new skills to meet today's challenges. Myles Munroe helps women to discover who they are. Whether you are a woman or a man, married or single, this book will help you to understand the woman as she was meant to be.

ISBN: 0-88368-671-6 • Trade • 192 pages

Understanding the Purpose and Power of Men
Dr. Myles Munroe

Today, the world is sending out conflicting signals about what it means to be a man. Many men are questioning who they are and what roles they fulfill in life-as a male, a husband, and a father. Best-selling author Myles Munroe examines cultural attitudes toward men and discusses the purpose God has given them. Discover the destiny and potential of the man as he was meant to be.

ISBN: 0-88368-725-9 • Trade • 224 pages

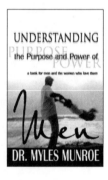

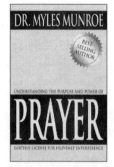

Understanding the Purpose and Power of Prayer
Dr. Myles Munroe

All that God is—and all that God has—may be received through prayer. Everything you need to fulfill your purpose on earth is available to you through prayer. The biblically-based, time-tested principles presented here will ignite and transform the way you pray. Be prepared to enter into a new dimension of faith, a deeper revelation of God's love, and a renewed understanding that your prayers can truly move the finger of God.

ISBN: 0-88368-442-X • Trade • 240 pages